WORLD HISTORY SERIES

The Battle of the Little Bighorn

Titles in the World History Series

The Age of Augustus
The Age of Feudalism
The Age of Pericles
The Alamo
America in the 1960s
The American Frontier
The American Revolution
Ancient Greece
The Ancient Near East
Architecture
Aztec Civilization
The Battle of the
    Little Bighorn
The Black Death
The Byzantine Empire
Caesar's Conquest of Gaul
The California Gold Rush
The Chinese Cultural
    Revolution
The Civil Rights Movement
The Collapse of the
    Roman Republic
The Conquest of Mexico
The Crimean War
The Crusades
The Cuban Missile Crisis
The Cuban Revolution
The Early Middle Ages
Egypt of the Pharaohs
Elizabethan England
The End of the Cold War
The French and Indian War
The French Revolution
The Glorious Revolution
The Great Depression
Greek and Roman
    Mythology
Greek and Roman Science

Greek and Roman Theater
The History of Slavery
Hitler's Reich
The Hundred Years' War
The Industrial Revolution
The Inquisition
The Italian Renaissance
The Late Middle Ages
The Lewis and Clark
    Expedition
The Mexican Revolution
The Mexican War of
    Independence
Modern Japan
The Mongol Empire
The Persian Empire
The Punic Wars
The Reformation
The Relocation of the
    North American Indian
The Renaissance
The Roaring Twenties
The Roman Empire
The Roman Republic
Roosevelt and the New Deal
The Russian Revolution
Russia of the Tsars
The Scientific Revolution
The Spread of Islam
The Stone Age
Traditional Africa
Traditional Japan
The Travels of Marco Polo
Twentieth Century Science
The Wars of the Roses
The Watts Riot
Women's Suffrage

WORLD HISTORY SERIES ■ ■ ■

The Battle of the Little Bighorn

by
Earle Rice Jr.

Lucent Books, P.O. Box 289011, San Diego, CA 92198-9011

Library of Congress Cataloging-in-Publication Data

Rice, Earle.
    The Battle of the Little Bighorn / by Earle Rice, Jr.
        p. cm. — (World history series)
    Includes bibliographical references and index.
    Summary: Describes the events leading up to, during, and
after the massacre of Custer's men by the Sioux in 1876.
    ISBN 1-56006-453-6 (alk. paper)
    1. Little Bighorn, Battle of the, Mont., 1876—Juvenile
literature. [1. Little Bighorn, Battle of the, Mont., 1876.]
I. Title. II. Series.
E83.876.R53   1998
973.8'2—dc21   97-9870
                                                        CIP
                                                         AC

Copyright 1998 by Lucent Books, Inc., P.O. Box 289011,
San Diego, California 92198-9011

Printed in the U.S.A.

Contents

Foreword   6

Important Dates in the History of
     the Battle of the Little Bighorn   8

INTRODUCTION
The Last Great Indian Victory   10

CHAPTER 1
Washita: Son of the Morning Star   12

CHAPTER 2
Custer: From Bull Run to the Black Hills   31

CHAPTER 3
Sitting Bull: Soldiers Falling into Camp   45

CHAPTER 4
Last Farewell: On to the Little Bighorn   55

CHAPTER 5
First Fight: Reno's Retreat   67

CHAPTER 6
Custer's Last Battle: A Sad and Terrible Blunder   77

EPILOGUE
Remembrances   89

Notes   93

Glossary   97

For Further Reading   99

Works Consulted   101

Index   106

Picture Credits   111

About the Author   112

Foreword

Each year on the first day of school, nearly every history teacher faces the task of explaining why his or her students should study history. One logical answer to this question is that exploring what happened in our past explains how the things we often take for granted—our customs, ideas, and institutions—came to be. As statesman and historian Winston Churchill put it, "Every nation or group of nations has its own tale to tell. Knowledge of the trials and struggles is necessary to all who would comprehend the problems, perils, challenges, and opportunities which confront us today." Thus, a study of history puts modern ideas and institutions in perspective. For example, though the founders of the United States were talented and creative thinkers, they clearly did not invent the concept of democracy. Instead, they adapted some democratic ideas that had originated in ancient Greece and with which the Romans, the British, and others had experimented. An exploration of these cultures, then, reveals their very real connection to us through institutions that continue to shape our daily lives.

Another reason often given for studying history is the idea that lessons exist in the past from which contemporary societies can benefit and learn. This idea, although controversial, has always been an intriguing one for historians. Those that agree that society can benefit from the past often quote philosopher George Santayana's famous statement, "Those who cannot remember the past are condemned to repeat it." Historians who ascribe to Santayana's philosophy believe that, for example, studying the events that led up to the major world wars or other significant historical events would allow society to chart a different and more favorable course in the future.

Just as difficult as convincing students to realize the importance of studying history is the search for useful and interesting supplementary materials that present historical events in a context that can be easily understood. The volumes in Lucent Books' World History Series attempt to present a broad, balanced, and penetrating view of the march of history. Ancient Egypt's important wars and rulers, for example, are presented against the rich and colorful backdrop of Egyptian religious, social, and cultural developments. The series engages the reader by enhancing historical events with these cultural contexts. For example, in *Ancient Greece*, the text covers the role of women in that society. Slavery is discussed in *The Roman Empire*, as well as how slaves earned their freedom. The numerous and varied aspects of everyday life in these and other societies are explored in each volume of the series. Additionally, the series covers the major political, cultural, and philosophical ideas as the torch of civilization is passed from ancient Mesopotamia and Egypt, through Greece, Rome, Medieval Europe, and other world cultures, to the modern day.

The material in the series is formatted in a thorough, precise, and organized manner. Each volume offers the reader a comprehensive and clearly written overview of an important historical event or period. The topic under discussion is placed in a broad historical context. For example, *The Italian Renaissance* begins with a discussion of the High Middle Ages and the loss of central control that allowed certain Italian cities to develop artistically. The book ends by looking forward to the Reformation and interpreting the societal changes that grew out of the Renaissance. Thus, students are not only involved in an historical era, but also enveloped by the events leading up to that era and the events following it.

One important and unique feature in the World History Series is the primary and secondary source quotations that richly supplement each volume. These quotes are useful in a number of ways. First, they allow students access to sources they would not normally be exposed to because of the difficulty and obscurity of the original source. The quotations range from interesting anecdotes to farsighted cultural perspectives and are drawn from historical witnesses both past and present. Second, the quotes demonstrate how and where historians themselves derive their information on the past as they strive to reach a consensus on historical events. Lastly, all of the quotes are footnoted, familiarizing students with the citation process and allowing them to verify quotes and/or look up the original source if the quote piques their interest.

Finally, the books in the World History Series provide a detailed launching point for further research. Each book contains a bibliography specifically geared toward student research. A second, annotated bibliography introduces students to all the sources the author consulted when compiling the book. A chronology of important dates gives students an overview, at a glance, of the topic covered. Where applicable, a glossary of terms is included.

In short, the series is designed not only to acquaint readers with the basics of history, but also to make them aware that their lives are a part of an ongoing human saga. Perhaps they will then come to the same realization as famed historian Arnold Toynbee. In his monumental work, *A Study of History,* he wrote about becoming aware of history flowing through him in a mighty current, and of his own life "welling like a wave in the flow of this vast tide."

Important Dates in the History of the Battle of the Little Bighorn

1864	1865	1866	1867	1868	1869

1864
September 30: General Custer assumes command of Third Cavalry Division.

1865
Spring: Custer-led cavalry spearheads final Union offensive in Shenandoah Valley, Virginia.

May 26: Civil War ends.

1868
November 27: Lieutenant Colonel George A. Custer leads cavalry attack on peaceful Cheyenne village at the Washita River in Indian Territory; 103 Indians killed; General

Sheridan's winter campaign begins.

1869–1873
Custer assigned to garrison duties in Fort Leavenworth, Kansas, and Elizabethtown, Kentucky.

1873
Spring: Custer leads Yellowstone Expedition into Dakota Territory.

September: Custer assumes command of Fort Abraham Lincoln, Dakota Territory.

1874
Summer: Custer leads Seventh Cavalry on Black Hills Expedition and discovers gold,

igniting gold rush into Indian lands.

1875
November 3: President Grant announces decision to make war against Indians.

December 3: Commissioner of Indian Affairs ordered to notify Indians to come into reservations by January 31, 1876, or be hunted down by the army and compelled to obey orders of Indian office.

1876
June 17: The Battle of the Rosebud; Indians force General George Crook's column to withdraw to base camp at Goose Creek.

June 22: Custer and the Seventh Cavalry depart from camp at mouth of the Rosebud; Gibbons (with Terry) resumes eastward march along the Yellowstone and Bighorn Rivers; rendezvous of two columns set for June 26 at the Little Bighorn River.

June 24: Custer arrives at the Little Bighorn.

June 25
Daybreak: Custer's scouts spot Indian smoke trails and ponies.

Late morning: Custer sends Captain Frederick W. Benteen's battalion on reconnaissance to left and south of main column.

2:30 P.M.: Forty Indians gallop off in front of Custer's column and head toward the Little Bighorn Valley; Custer orders Major Marcus A. Reno's battalion to pursue Indians across Little Bighorn and attack camp.

3:45 P.M.: Chief Gall and Crazy Horse attack Custer at the Little Bighorn; Custer and five companies wiped out to the man; Benteen hooks up with Reno on Reno Hill.

4:55 P.M.– 5:45 P.M.: Benteen and Reno forces attempting to aid Custer turn back at Weir Point and dig in on Reno Hill.

June 26: Reno and Benteen besieged on Reno Hill.

June 27: Terry and Gibbons arrive at the Little Bighorn; Indians withdraw to the south.

June 30: Wounded survivors of Reno-Benteen siege evacuated aboard the river steamer *Far West*.

The Last Great Indian Victory

On June 25, 1876, the day of the Battle of the Little Bighorn, the Sioux and Cheyenne won a startling victory over the white man's horse soldiers. The shocking army casualties for the entire battle totaled 263 killed (212 with Custer), 59 wounded, and 25 missing (4 Crow and 21 Arikara scouts, all of whom survived). All of the Seventh Cavalry column under Custer's immediate command were killed. Because the Indi-

Sioux and Cheyenne warriors rout Custer's Seventh Cavalry during the Battle of the Little Bighorn on June 25, 1876.

ans kept no records, the numbers of their dead and wounded will remain forever undetermined. Lieutenant Edward S. Godfrey wrote:

> The loss of the Hostiles has never been determined. Thirty-eight dead were found in the village, one at Reno Hill and on the reconnaissance up the Little Big Horn valley, numerous bodies were found sepultured [laid to rest] in trees and on scaffolds. They had no statistics of their dead and wounded.[1]

The Indians, partially out of battlefield custom and partially for revenge, used knives to mutilate many of the corpses. The soldiers that found the remains of Custer and his cavalry found pools of dried blood near Custer's head. After the battle, some Cheyenne women had recognized Custer, whom the Indians called "Yellow Hair" and "Son of the Morning Star." The women punctured his eardrums with long needles several times. Years before, the Cheyennes had warned Custer that if he continued to attack the Indians, he would die. He had not listened. Now, the women tried to clear out his ears so that he would hear better in the afterlife.

At Little Bighorn, the followers of Sitting Bull, Crazy Horse, and others won a great battle but, ironically, lost the war. Custer's defeat—and the sheer savagery of the battle's aftermath—enraged the American public. Their clamor for revenge would not be stilled until the last Indian was forced to surrender. Most of the nontreaty Indians surrendered to white authorities within the next year and allowed themselves to be confined to reservations. A few led by Sitting Bull found brief sanctuary in Canada, but they too gave up in 1881.

The Sioux Wars ended—and with them a way of life.

1 Washita: Son of the Morning Star

By the time of the Battle of the Little Bighorn Colonel George A. Custer had participated many times on the battlefield. Under the leadership of General Winfield Scott Hancock, Custer led the Seventh Cavalry in pursuit of the mobile and elusive Sioux and Cheyennes in 1867. Custer, a charismatic young officer with long, flowing hair, boasted an enviable record of gallantry and advancement. During the Civil War, he had attained the wartime rank of major general. Reduced to a peacetime rank of lieutenant colonel after the war, Custer welcomed the chance to recover past glories in his first frontier command. But fate frowned on his first efforts.

The exhausting campaign stretched across the central plains from April through July. To Custer's long-enduring frustration, the chase ended in another ineffective and expensive failure for an army too small and ill equipped for the task.

On August 1, fighting broke out again along the Bozeman Trail, an emigrant route from Julesburg, Colorado, to the Virginia goldfields in Montana. The Teton Sioux resented the trail because it cut across the Indian hunting preserve and sustained an ongoing stream of wagon trains. In the so-called Hayfield Fight, the Sioux attacked a group of hay cutters in a field near Fort C. F. Smith, one of three forts built to protect travelers. Another band of Sioux struck a party of woodcutters the next day near Fort Phil Kearny in the Wagon Box Fight (so named because the troopers fought from within a makeshift refuge formed by wagon bodies, or boxes).

The dashing young George Armstrong Custer earned a reputation for bravery during the Civil War. After the war, Custer pursued a career on the frontier.

Comanche and Kiowa chiefs sign the Medicine Lodge treaties, which established two reservations for the Southern Plains Indians.

By this time, the army had replaced the awkward muzzle-loading rifles used earlier with more efficient breech loaders. With their new faster-fire capability, the troopers inflicted heavy casualties on the surprised Indians and forced them to withdraw. They would return another day.

Broken Treaties

In Washington, the mounting costs and successive failures resulting from the campaigns against the Indians spurred a new peace movement. Government peace commissioners negotiated two sets of treaties with the Indians; the first, with the Southern Plains Indians at Medicine Lodge Creek, Kansas, in the fall of 1867; the second, with the Northern Plains Indians at Fort Laramie, Wyoming, in the spring of 1868.

The Medicine Lodge treaties established two large reservations in Indian Territory (now Oklahoma); one for the

Cheyennes and Arapahos; another for the Kiowas, Comanches, and the Kiowa-Apaches. As part of the treaties, the Indians were to receive clothing and other amenities while changing their lifestyles from hunting to farming. The government recognized the need to supply food to the Indians in the interim but did not include provisions for such necessities in the treaties.

The treaty signed at Fort Laramie the following spring ended the War for the Bozeman Trail and Hancock's Campaign. The Laramie Treaty of 1868 began on a hopeful note:

> From this day forward all war between the parties to this agreement shall forever cease. The Government of the United States desires peace, and its honor is hereby pledged to keep it. The Indians desire peace, and they now pledge their honor to maintain it.[2]

Briefly, the Laramie Treaty designated the Powder River country as "unceded Indian territory"[3]; set up the Great Sioux

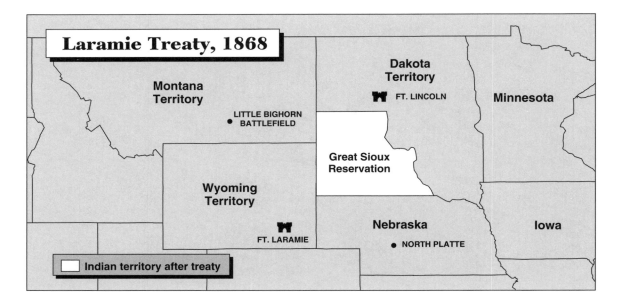

Laramie Treaty, 1868

Montana Territory

LITTLE BIGHORN BATTLEFIELD

Dakota Territory

🚂 FT. LINCOLN

Minnesota

Great Sioux Reservation

Wyoming Territory

🚂 FT. LARAMIE

Nebraska

● NORTH PLATTE

Iowa

☐ Indian territory after treaty

Reservation west of the Missouri River in what is now South Dakota; granted hunting privileges outside the reservation "so long as the buffalo may range thereon in such numbers as to justify the chase"[4]; and called for the abandonment of all the forts along the Bozeman Trail. Despite the treaty, roving bands of Dog Soldiers—Indian mercenaries of a sort—continued to raid.

Historically, Indians often signed treaties with little or no idea as to their terms. The lack of any clear understanding of a treaty's provisions proved unimportant when considering that such terms were seldom kept and that most treaties were soon broken.

In February 1868, after failing to receive food supplies as promised by the government (although not a treaty requirement), the Kiowas and Comanches fled the reservation and started raiding settlements in Texas. The Cheyennes commenced similar forays along the Saline and Solomon Rivers in Kansas. These Indian excursions off the reservation prompted the government to discard its peace movement in favor of a more aggressive policy.

Sheridan's Winter Campaign

General William Tecumseh Sherman, commander of the army's vast Division of the Missouri, declared, "These Indians require to be soundly whipped, and the ringleaders in the present trouble hung, their ponies killed, and such destruction of their property as will make them very poor."[5] Sherman then selected General Philip Henry Sheridan, his subordinate and commander of the Department of the Missouri, to implement his declaration. "Go ahead in your own way," Sherman said, "and I will back you with my full authority."[6]

Sheridan shared his superior's views and started planning at once for a winter campaign, noting:

If [a winter campaign] results in the utter annihilation of these Indians, it is but the result of what they have been warned again and again. . . . I will say nothing and do nothing to restrain our troops from doing what they deem proper on the spot, and will allow no mere vague general charges of cruelty and inhumanity to tie their hands.[7]

While Sheridan planned a winter campaign, the Indians struck first in the autumn of 1868, at the Arikara Fork of the Republican River in western Kansas.

During September 17–24, a war party of six to seven hundred Oglala Sioux and Dog Soldiers laid siege to a patrol of fifty plainsmen commanded by Major George A. Forsyth. Armed with repeating carbines, Forsyth's troopers managed to hold off the Indians for eight days. A relief column finally arrived from Fort Wallace—some ninety miles distant—to drive away the attackers. Forsyth had by then lost half of his force in killed or wounded to the rampaging Sioux.

Sheridan's winter campaign called for a three-pronged thrust against the Indians of the southern plains. One column would march east from Fort Bascom, New Mexico; the second was to slant southeast from Fort Lyon, Colorado; while the third and largest, under Custer, would move south from Fort Dodge, Kansas. The plan intended for all three columns to converge on the Indians' winter camps on the Canadian and Washita Rivers in Indian Territory.

By assigning command of the dominant column to Custer, Sheridan showed great confidence in the colorful cavalry officer who had served as one of his favorite young lieutenants during the Civil War. Eager to allay the frustrations of his earlier, fruitless operations against the Sioux and Cheyennes, Custer set his mind to do whatever it took to justify Sheridan's faith in him. Nor did the potential for enhancing his reputation as a premier Indian-fighter elude him as he followed the trumpet's call into the wilderness of the southern plains.

When treaties between the U.S. government and the Indian nations failed to bring peace, General Philip Sheridan was called upon to pursue the renegade Indians and force them back on the reservations.

The Battle of the Washita gave both name and fame to Custer as an Indian-fighter. Shortly before daybreak on November 27, 1868, the flamboyant "boy general"[8] positioned eleven troops (companies) of the Seventh Cavalry—about eight hundred troopers in all—on four sides of Black Kettle's sleeping Cheyenne

---

Dog Soldiers

The Hotamitanio, or Dog Soldiers, were members of an elite warrior clique among the Cheyenne and various other tribes of the western plains. As members of this inner "soldier society," their principal duties consisted of policing tribe activities, such as ceremonies, hunts, and raiding parties. Some even appear to have functioned as mercenaries—soldiers for hire—in the service of a specific chief or group. For their role as enforcers, their fellow tribe members treated the Dog Soldiers with great respect and rewarded them with privileges beyond the common measure.

By 1837, the Dog Soldiers had become a separate militant band within the Cheyenne tribe. They later exhibited great prowess in combat and achieved fame or notoriety, as determined by one's personal bias, during the Cheyenne-Arapaho War. Led by Chiefs Tall Bull, Bull Bear, and White Horse during this violent period, the Dog Soldiers succeeded in countering the more peaceable chiefs in their attempts to achieve harmony with the white man. Notable among the chiefs seeking peace was the hapless Black Kettle, who escaped Chivington's raid at Sand Creek, Colorado, only to be slain four years later by the Seventh Cavalry at the Washita River.

Many historians have portrayed the Dog Soldiers as murdering savages and in other equally unflattering terms. Tom LeForge, who lived twenty-two years with the Crows, offered a more moderate description. He asserted that the Dog Soldiers were just cops, "the immediate directors of conduct." But the very name Dog Soldier stirred the creative fires of some romantically inclined historians. To imaginative writers the name implied "the utmost of wild ferocity, so the orderly home policemen had attributed to them, especially, many of the gory deeds done by the Indians who resisted the movement of emigrants across the plains."

Under Tall Bull, the Dog Soldiers resisted confinement on a reservation until they were finally subdued by the Fifth Cavalry on July 11, 1869. Two hundred and fifty troopers and fifty allied Pawnees surprised the Dog Soldiers in their camp at Summit Springs, Colorado, killing Tall Bull and achieving total victory.

Hostile Indians prepare to attack a white settlement. The U.S. government justified its new aggressive Indian policy by pointing to these unprovoked attacks on settlers.

village. Custer and his troopers had struggled across sixty miles of snow-covered country, from Camp Supply, Kansas, to the Washita River in Indian Territory. The soldiers had endured the ravages of blizzards and sub-zero temperatures to arrive at their destination at 10:00 P.M. on November 26. Their trek had begun three days earlier at Camp Supply, a newly established base camp about a mile from the junction of Wolf and Beaver Creeks in southwestern Kansas. Their reasons for venturing farther into hostile Indian country than had any white soldiers before them can be traced back to the previous summer.

A New Indian Policy

During the summer of 1868, repeated raids on white settlements by belligerent factions of the Cheyennes and Arapahos convinced General Sherman that treaties made earlier with the Indians had failed to keep order on the plains. Sherman decided that stronger measures were needed. In a passionate message to Secretary of War John M. Schofield, the general stated:

> All the Cheyennes and Arapahoes are now at war. Admitting that some have not done acts of murder, rape, etc., still they have not restrained those who have; nor have they on demand given up the criminals as they agreed to do. The treaty made at Medicine-Lodge [in 1867] is, therefore, already broken by them. . . . No better time could be possibly chosen than the present for destroying or humiliating those bands that have so outrageously violated their treaties & begun a devastating war without one particle of provocation; and after a reasonable

General William Sherman, an outspoken opponent of the Indians, advocated a "war with vindictive earnestness against all hostile Indians, till they are obliterated or beg for mercy."

time given for the innocent to withdraw, I will solicit an order from the President declaring all Indians who remain outside their lawful reservations to be outlaws, and commanding all people—soldiers & citizens—to proceed against them as such.[9]

President Ulysses S. Grant approved Sherman's subsequent request to initiate a new Indian policy, concurring that "Our settlements, etc., must be protected—even if the extermination of every Indian tribe is necessary to secure such a result."[10] Sherman then vowed strong action against the Indians.

"I will urge Gen'l Sheridan to push his measures for the utter destruction and subjugation of all who are outside [the reservation] in a hostile attitude," Sher-man informed Grant and Schofield. "I propose that he shall prosecute the war with vindictive earnestness against all hostile Indians, till they are obliterated or beg for mercy."[11] General Sheridan left no doubt as to where he stood on the Indian situation.

"The only good Indians I ever saw were dead!"[12] Sheridan said. Sherman, of course, could not have agreed more:

> Yes; and the more we can kill this year, the less we'll have to kill next year. For the more I see of these [expletive] red devils, the more convinced I am that they have to be killed or be maintained as a species of paupers. Their attempts at civilization are simply ridiculous. We have tried kindness, till it is construed as weakness. Now we must deal with them on their own terms.[13]

Sheridan needed a proven leader to help him deal with the Indians "on their own terms." He decided on George Armstrong Custer. At that time, however, Custer was serving a one-year suspension from duty for leaving camp without proper authorization and for treating deserters harshly. Sheridan appealed at once to Washington for Custer's reinstatement.

Back in the Saddle

On September 24, 1868, Sheridan sent a telegram to Monroe, Michigan, summoning Custer's return to duty:

> Generals Sherman, [Brigadier General Alfred] Sully, and myself, and nearly all of your regiment have asked for you, and I hope the application [for

reinstatement] will be successful. Can you come at once? Eleven companies of your regiment will move out about the 1st of October against the hostile Indians, from Medicine Lodge Creek, toward the Wichita Mountains.[14]

Custer bade a quick farewell to his wife, Libbie, and boarded a westbound train the next morning, trusting to his unerring luck that Washington would approve his reinstatement. Three days later, General Sheridan welcomed Custer's arrival at Fort Hays in central Kansas. Sheridan, over breakfast, briefed his former lieutenant on his plans for a winter campaign.

Sheridan figured that the heavy winter snows would hinder the Indians from moving very far or fast. If the army could raze the Indian villages and destroy their supplies, the Indians would then be forced to come into the reservations or starve. Sheridan concluded the briefing with his first directions for Custer:

> Custer, I rely on you in everything, and shall send you on this expedition without orders, leaving you to act entirely on your own judgment.[15]

Custer left Fort Hays on October 4 and rejoined his regiment two days later at Fort Dodge, Kansas, seventy-five miles southwest of Fort Hays on the Arkansas River. Custer was back in the saddle.

No Task Too Great

At Fort Dodge, in addition to eleven troops of his own Seventh Cavalry, Custer found five companies of Brigadier General Alfred Sully's Third U.S. Infantry.

Moreover, General Sheridan had ordered the Nineteenth Kansas Volunteer Cavalry to join the column in November at a soon-to-be-established base camp. The Nineteenth Cavalry was a poorly trained and ill-equipped group of volunteers, organized at Topeka and commanded by former Kansas governor Colonel Samuel J. Crawford. Sully's column of infantry and some four hundred wagons, with Custer's cavalry in the lead, left Fort Dodge on November 12. Six days later, at a favorable site seventy-five miles southwest of Fort Dodge, the column halted and the soldiers began construction of a fortified base camp that soon took the name of Camp Supply.

The expected arrival of Crawford's volunteers sparked a clash over rank and overall command authority between Sully and Custer. In lineal rank, that is, permanent peacetime rank, both officers were lieutenant colonels. But in brevet rank, or temporary wartime rank, Sully was a brigadier general, while Custer held the next higher rank of major general. An army regulation called for the highest

A view of Camp Supply, the fortified base camp built by the cavalry troops during the winter campaign.

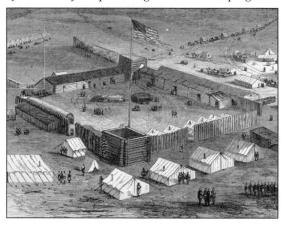

brevet rank to take effect in commands or detachments "composed of different corps."[16] When General Sheridan arrived at Camp Supply with last-minute orders for Sully and Custer, he implemented that regulation by placing Custer in command. Sheridan then directed Custer to

> proceed south in the direction of the Antelope Hills, thence toward the Washita River, the supposed winter seat of the hostile tribes, to destroy their villages and ponies, to kill or hang all warriors, and bring back all women and children.[17]

Sheridan's plans for a winter campaign had prompted an earlier comment from Jim Bridger, a well-known pioneer and Indian scout: "You can't hunt Injuns on the Plains in winter for blizzards don't respect man or beast."[18] Custer disagreed:

> All the better for us! We can move; the Indians can't. If we attempted to fight 'em in a warmer season, as was our old mistake, we should yield to them the advantage of climate and supplies, of bountiful forage for their ponies, immense herds of game for their war parties, allowing them to move freely from point to point. We should then be meeting them on ground of their own selection. Winter will hold them down for the kill.[19]

After defending Sheridan's strategy, Custer then persuaded his superior to leave Sully's infantry behind.

"They'll only hamper our progress in tracking the hostiles," Custer explained, "and I'm firmly confident the 7th Cavalry is equal to any band of Indians on the Plains."[20] Nor did Custer want the company of Crawford's ill-trained volunteers.

Pleading for them to be left behind, he said, "The 7th can handle anything it meets."[21]

With a nod, Sheridan said, "I believe it can. The field is entirely yours."[22] Custer beamed with pleasure and confidence. No task was too great for his invincible Seventh Cavalry.

Misery and Danger Ahead

On Sunday evening, November 22, Custer scribbled a hurried letter to his dear Libbie, who was temporarily quartered at Fort Leavenworth, Kansas:

> Some of the officers think this may be a campaign on paper—but I know Genl. Sheridan better. We are going to the heart of Indian country where white troops have never been before.[23]

A fierce blizzard struck the plains that night, depositing more than a foot of snow on the ground by morning. When Custer went to bid farewell to General Sheridan shortly after daybreak, Sheridan asked him what he thought about the storm. Custer replied that it was very much to his liking. He later wrote:

> If the snow only remained on the ground one week, I promised to bring the General satisfactory evidences that my command had met the Indians. With an earnest injunction from my chief to keep him informed, if possible, should anything important occur, and many hearty wishes for a successful issue to the campaign, I bade him adieu.[24]

Undeterred by the snow, Custer and the Seventh Cavalry begin their march into hostile territory.

It was still snowing when Custer mounted his horse and shouted to his command: "Seventh Cavalry, by column of twos, forward *ho!*" With the regimental band blaring the jaunty strains of "The Girl I Left Behind Me," Custer led his troopers out of Camp Supply and into a blinding snowstorm. Ahead lay the promise of misery and danger in a hostile land where no white soldier had gone before.

"We Attack at Dawn"

The column trekked about fifteen miles the first day and reached Wolf Creek at two o'clock that afternoon. By then the wagon train had fallen far behind and the troopers set up camp for the night. Under clear skies the next day, November 24, the column persevered through snow now about eighteen inches deep. Many of the soldiers became snow-blinded by the bright sun reflecting off the glistening snow. Horses struggled with snow balling on their feet

and causing them to flounder and tire quickly with the added exertion. Still, the column covered another eighteen miles.

November 25 found the column still moving westerly along Wolf Creek, then turning south toward the Canadian River. The soldiers could now see the jagged outline of the Antelope Hills on the horizon and guided on them for the rest of the day. Late that evening, they set up camp about a mile from the Canadian River. Cold, saddle sore, and exhausted, the troopers welcomed sleep.

At daybreak on November 26, Major Joel H. Elliott, commanding troops G, H, and M, spotted an Indian trail in the snow that had been made by an estimated one hundred warriors. The tracks, although partially covered by snow, appeared to have been made within the past twenty-four hours. Custer ordered Elliott and his troops to follow the trail in advance of the main column until 9:00 P.M., then wait for the rest of the column to catch up.

Elliott departed and Custer prepared to follow him as quickly as possible. He assigned eighty troopers to stay with the wagons and ordered the rest to strip to the bare combat essentials. Each soldier was armed with a Spencer metallic cartridge magazine carbine and a Colt .44 revolver, and each carried one hundred rounds of ammunition, as well as coffee, hard bread, and an overcoat. Their blankets were left behind with the wagons.

Traveling light, Custer's main column caught up with Elliott at 9:00 P.M. The soldiers unsaddled their mounts and rested for an hour in a wooded area near a stream. They hit the trail again an hour later. Indian trackers Little Beaver and Hard Rope led the way, a half mile in advance of the regiment. Custer trailed right behind his trackers. After tracking another three hours, Little Beaver reined up suddenly. Custer asked, "What is the matter?" Little Beaver answered, "Me don't know, but me smell fire." Custer and his trackers rode ahead to the crest of a small rise. By then the moon had risen, illuminating the valley below. Little Beaver whispered, "Heaps Injuns down there."[25] But Custer could see only what looked like a large body of animals. He asked Little Beaver why he thought there were Indians down there.

"Me heard dog bark,"[26] the tracker replied.

Custer remained unconvinced. The two men waited silently for another sound that might indicate the presence of Black Kettle's clan. Several moments later, they heard the faint tinkling of a bell, indicative of an Indian pony herd. Then the unmistakable cry of an infant rang out and echoed across the valley on the cold, thin air. Custer needed no more convincing. He looked at Little Beaver and said, "We attack at dawn."[27]

Plan of Attack

Custer returned to his column, summoned his officers, and outlined his plan of attack. He later wrote:

> The general plan was to employ the hours between then [about midnight] and daylight to completely surround the village and at daybreak, or as soon as it was barely light enough for the purpose, to attack the Indians from all sides. The command, numbering . . . about eight hundred mounted men, was divided into four nearly equal detachments. Two of them set out at once, as they had to make a circuitous march of several miles in order to arrive at the points assigned them from which to make their attack. The third detachment moved to its position about an hour before day, and until that time remained with the main or fourth column. These last, whose movements I accompanied, were to make the attack from the point from which we had first discovered the herd and the village. Major Elliot[t] commanded the column embracing G, H, and M troops, Seventh Cavalry, which moved around from our left to a position almost in the rear of the village; while Colonel Thompson commanded the one consisting of B and F troops, which moved in a corresponding manner from our right to a position which was to connect with that of Major Elliot[t]. Colonel Meyers commanded the third column, composed of E and I troops, which was to take position in the valley and timber a little less than a mile to my right.[28]

Custer envisioned that this deployment would effectively block the escape of everyone in the village. He continued:

> That portion of the command which I proposed to accompany consisted of A, C, D, and K troops, Seventh Cavalry, the Osages [Indian trackers] and scouts, and Colonel [William W.] Cooke and his forty sharpshooters. Captain Hamilton commanded one of the squadrons, Colonel [Robert M.] West the other. After the first two columns had departed for their posts—it was still four hours before the hour of attack—the men of the other two columns were permitted to dismount, but much intense suffering was unavoidably sustained.[29]

Once in position, the soldiers awaited the dawn—and orders to attack the unsuspecting Cheyennes. The night grew bitterly cold. The men covered their heads with their overcoat capes and crouched in whatever shelter they could find to protect themselves against the icy winter winds. They could not even stamp their feet or clap their arms to keep warm for fear of attracting unwanted attention from village dogs. Custer himself huddled on buffalo robes with a pack of staghounds and stole an hour of sleep.

Star of Wonder

Custer awakened about two hours before dawn and saw a bright ball of golden light ascending in the already lightening eastern sky. Awesome in its swelling size and brilliance, everyone stared unknowingly at the rising sphere, as if hypnotized in the presence of some kind of divine light. All eyes watched the mysterious ball of light as it moved closer and closer toward Custer and his men. "Bejaysus," gasped California Joe, one of Custer's white scouts. "How long it hangs fire. Why don't it explode?"

"What is it anyhow?" asked another white scout.

"No mystery, gentlemen," Custer replied, peering at the sparkling phenomenon. "You are now looking at the brightest and most beautiful of morning stars."[30]

Immediately preceding the dawn and the start of one of Seventh Cavalry's most important battles, the so-called Star of Washita excited the "anxiety and alarm"[31] of Custer and his troopers. Whether they welcomed the star's timely arrival as a good omen remains shrouded in romantic conjecture. Perhaps even less is known about the Indians' perception of that predawn phenomenon. Yet, to this day, when Cheyennes gather around tribal fires and exchange tales about Washita, they speak of Custer as "Son of the Morning Star."[32]

A Classic Charge

The star's intensity faded in the morning sky. Custer's men advanced on the sleeping village from four directions. Captain Albert Barnitz, one of the attackers, recalled:

> We had just reached the edge of a shallow ravine beyond which we could see the clustered teepees, situated among wide-branching cottonwood

The Indian Scout

The Indian scout played a vital part in the U.S. Cavalry's campaign against the Plains Indians. In his book My Life on the Plains, *General George A. Custer, an accomplished writer, described the character and role of a typical frontier scout.*

"It is usual on the Plains, and particularly during time of active hostilities, for every detachment of troops to be accompanied by one or more professional scouts or guides. These guides are employed by the government at a rate of compensation far in excess of that paid to the soldiers, some of the most experienced receiving pay about equal to that of a subaltern [junior officer] in the line. They constitute a most interesting as well as useful and necessary portion of our frontier population. . . .

They are almost invariably men of very superior judgment or common sense, with education generally better than that of the average frontiersman. Their most striking characteristics are love of adventure, a natural and cultivated knowledge of the country without recourse to maps, deep hatred of the Indian and an intimate acquaintance with all the habits and customs of the latter, whether pertaining to peace or war, and last but most necessary to their calling skill in the use of firearms and in the management of a horse. The possessor of these qualifications and more than the ordinary amount of courage may feel equal to discharge the dangerous and trying duties of a scout. . . .

Scouts usually prefer a good mule to a horse, and wisely too, for the reason that in making perilous journeys, either singly or by twos or threes, celerity [swiftness] is one principal condition to success. The object with the scout is not to outrun or overwhelm the Indians, but to avoid both by secrecy and caution in his movements. . . . The mule will perform [as a horse will not] a rapid and continuous march without forage [food], being able to subsist on the grazing to be obtained in nearly all the valleys on the Plains during the greater portion of the year."

trees, when a shot was fired in the village, and instantly we heard the band on the ridge beyond it strike up the familiar air "Garry Owen" and the answering cheers of the men, as Custer and his legion came thundering down the long divide, while nearer at hand on our right came Benteen's squadron, crashing through the frozen snow, as the troops deployed into line at a gallop, and the Indian village rang with war-whoops, the quick discharge of fire-arms, the clamorous barking of dogs, the cries of infants and the wailing of women.[33]

The long-haired Custer, locks unfurled to the winter wind, led his galloping horsemen in a classic cavalry charge against the startled Indians. Most of the Indians would soon be dead.

A Lasting Impression

Captain Louis Hamilton, the grandson of Alexander Hamilton, took a bullet in the heart during the charge. A fellow officer saw Hamilton jerk and twitch in his saddle before he "stiffened in his stirrups and was thus carried a corpse for a distance of several yards, when he fell from his horse."[34]

Captain Barnitz fell when a bullet pierced his overcoat and lodged in his stomach. Thinking himself dying, he dictated a "last" letter to his wife while awaiting death at a field hospital: "Tell Mrs. B that I don't regret the wound so much as I do leaving her. It has been so long since we met, that the expectations of the happiness we would enjoy upon our reunion is more than I can bear."[35] But death

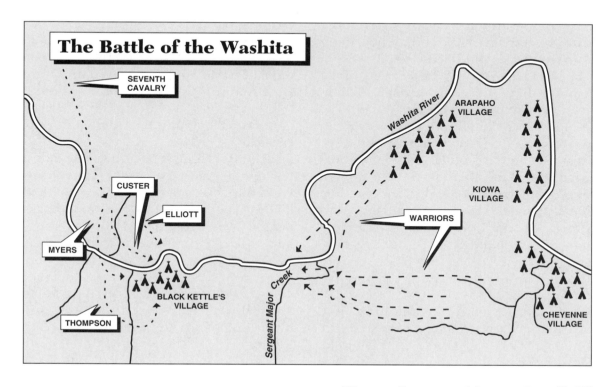

The Battle of the Washita

Custer (left) and his troopers descend upon the unsuspecting Cheyennes during the Battle of the Washita. The bloody attack claimed the lives of 103 Indians.

passed him by at Washita. Interestingly, when Barnitz died years later at the age of seventy-seven, an autopsy revealed a growth around his 1868 bullet wound as the cause of death.

Women and children fought along with the warriors. One Indian boy about fourteen years old fired several shots at Captain Frederick W. Benteen. One of the boy's bullets pierced the neck of Benteen's horse, leaving the officer with no option except to kill the boy. Nearby, an old woman dragged a captive white boy into a protective gully. When troopers tried to reclaim the boy, the old woman drew a butcher knife and sliced open the boy's stomach. Lieutenant Thomas Ward Custer, George's brother, took a random bullet in the hand. And George's favorite staghound, Blucher, fell dead, speared through by an arrow while chasing some fleeing Indians.

In another confrontation, some Indians attacked several ammunition and supply wagons led by Quartermaster James M. Bell. Bell's wagons made it through to Custer with the ammunition, but Bell had been forced to abandon much-needed blankets and other supplies.

At the height of the frenzied action, Major Elliott sighted a group of warriors escaping downstream on foot. He quickly gathered a group of volunteer troopers to give chase. Elliott wheeled in his saddle, waved his hat toward Lieutenant Owen Hale standing close by, and shouted: "Here goes for a brevet or a coffin."[36] Hale never saw Elliott and the volunteer troopers again.

The fight in the village lasted only a few minutes, but the troopers spent several hours flushing out warriors who had fled to sheltering gullies and underbrush nearby. By late afternoon, Custer's troops had killed 103 Indians, including Black Kettle and his wife, shot while riding double on a pony, trying to escape. Bodies of animals and Indians alike lay scattered all about the village. Women, children, and old people made up ninety-three of the Cheyenne dead. Custer then ordered the village razed and the Indian pony herd

The Battle of the Washita

On November 27, 1868, Brevet Major General George A. Custer, a cavalry officer already renowned for his gallantry and flamboyance during the Civil War, began blazing a name for himself on the western frontier. By destroying Cheyenne chief Black Kettle's camp and most of its inhabitants, Custer served notice to the Plains Indians that a new and formidable foe had arrived in Indian Territory to enforce the white man's rule. Custer's notes on the Washita battle provide interesting insights into the general's own perception of his first major clash with the Indians.

"Accessions to our opponents [Indian reinforcements] kept arriving, mounted warriors in full war-panoply, with floating lance pennants . . . Cheyennes, Arapahoes, Kiowas, Comanches, and some Apaches, hostile tribes from some twelve miles off. . . .

From being the surrounding party we now found ourselves surrounded, Indians on all sides closing in on us.

Help arrived, a fresh supply of ammunition with which the Quartermaster, Major Bell, by heroic efforts had contrived to reach us. Despite their vast numerical superiority the Indians fought with less confidence than their wont [usual way]. . . . Vain their efforts to draw us from the village. We applied the torch to this with all the captured property.

I was now determined to take the offensive. It was about three in the afternoon. . . . I knew that the officers in charge of the [supply] train and eighty men would be following us on the trail, and feared that the Indians, reconnoitring [surveying] from hilltops, might discover this helpless detachment, and annihilate them, at the same time leaving the command in mid-winter, in the heart of enemy country, destitute of provision for horse and man. . . .

Eight hundred and seventy ponies, wild, unused to white man's control, were on our hands. Such wealth, from the Indian standpoint, would cause us to be waylaid, night and day. This, with sixty prisoners [women and children] to convey, our own wounded to care for, the exhausted condition of our troops, might have resulted in the loss of all we had gained. Having caused the best ponies to be selected for our captives, I issued an order as painful to decide on as to carry out—that the unwanted ponies should be shot."

destroyed. His troops torched seventy-five village teepees and slew almost nine hundred Indian ponies.

The ponies, although of no use to the Seventh Cavalry, could not be left to be used later against the soldiers. Furthermore, the destruction of the ponies was intended to send a message to the Indians, as Custer explained later:

> If we retained them they [the Indians] might conclude that one object of our expedition against them was to secure plunder, an object thoroughly consistent with the red man's idea of war. Instead, it was our desire to impress upon his uncultured mind that our every act and purpose had been simply to inflict deserved punishment upon him for the many murders and depredations committed by him in and around the homes of defenseless settlers on the frontier.[37]

It seems safe to say that Custer and the Seventh Cavalry made a lasting—if less than humane—impression on the Indians that day at Washita.

Gallant Services Rendered

As the shadows lengthened across the valley, the unexpected arrival of Indian reinforcements threatened to turn Custer's easy victory into a humbling defeat. Always as impulsive as he was daring, Custer had failed before attacking to properly reconnoiter the area for the possible presence of other Indians. Late in the afternoon, he found himself and his command

Following the Battle of the Washita, Custer's command destroyed nearly nine hundred Indian ponies to prevent them from being used in future battles, as well as to further punish the Indians.

The Naked and the Dead

"Fort Cobb, Indian Territory, Dec. 22, 1868 On the 11th we camped within a few miles of our "battle of the Washita," and Gens. Sheridan and Custer, with a detail of one hundred men, mounted, as escort, went out with the view of searching for the bodies of our nineteen comrades, including Maj. Elliott.

The bodies were found in a small circle, stripped as naked as when born, and frozen still. Their heads had been battered in, and some of them had been entirely chopped off; some of them had had the Adam's apple cut out of their throats; some had their hands and feet cut off, and nearly all had been horribly mangled in a way delicacy forbids me to mention. They lay scarcely two miles from the scene of the fight, and all we knew of the manner they were killed we have learned from Indian sources. It seems that Maj. Elliott's party was pursuing a well-mounted party of Cheyennes in the direction of the Grand Village, where nearly all the tribes were encamped, and were surrounded by reinforcements coming to the rescue of the pursued, before the Major was aware of their position. . . . As soon as Maj. Elliott found that he was surrounded he caused his men to dismount, and did some execution among the Indians, which added to the mortification they must have felt at the loss of the village and herds of their friends and allies, and enraged them so that they determined upon the destruction of the entire little band. . . .

Round and round rush the red fiends, smaller and smaller shrinks the circle, but the aim of that devoted, gallant knot of heroes is steadier than ever. . . . Soon every voice in the little band is still as death; but the hellish work of the savages is scarce begun, and their ingenuities are taxed to invent barbarities to practice on the bodies of the fallen brave."

almost besieged by many additional warriors from camps beyond the nearby hills. But Custer held position against the counterattacking Indians.

Custer waited until dark; then, with banners flying and the band blaring "Garry Owen," brazenly marched his troops downstream as if to attack the distant Indian camps. Although outnumbering the troopers, the Indians overestimated Custer's strength in the face of such boldness and called off their counterattack. While the Indians withdrew to defend their villages, the Seventh Cavalry slipped safely out of the valley in the sheltering darkness.

The regiment returned to Camp Supply, where Sheridan hailed Custer's attack at Washita as a great victory and proof of the effectiveness of Sheridan's winter-campaign strategy. Custer won personal acclaim but at an ugly cost to the Seventh Cavalry: five troopers killed and fourteen wounded, plus nineteen missing.

The missing troopers were Major Elliott and his volunteers, all of whose mutilated corpses were found two weeks later. Much has been written about why Custer withdrew his main column without attempting a thorough search for his missing troopers. Before faulting Custer's action, critics should first consider his circumstances. Custer faced a superior force, in unfamiliar territory, and under severe weather conditions. His supply wagons stood virtually unprotected several miles away. The loss of his supplies might also mean the loss of his ill-clad regiment to the icy elements. A field commander's first responsibility is the safety of his entire command. Regrettably, Elliott and his troopers perished, but Custer brought most of his regiment back to camp safely. In this important sense, Custer acted correctly.

In a report of the Washita expedition issued to General Sherman on November 29, General Sheridan reaffirmed his praise for Custer. The report concluded:

> The energy and rapidity shown during one of the heaviest snow-storms that has visited this section of the country, with the temperature below the freezing point, and the gallantry and bravery displayed, resulting in such signal success, reflect the highest credit upon both the officers and men of the Seventh Cavalry; and the Major-General commanding [Sheridan] . . . desires to express his thanks to the officers and men engaged in the battle of the Washita, and his special congratulations to their distinguished commander, Brevet Major-General G. A. Custer, for the efficient and gallant services rendered.[38]

The Son of the Morning Star, like his namesake, had established himself as a bright new star on the western frontier.

2 Custer: From Bull Run to the Black Hills

Few military careers lend stronger support to the argument that heroes are born rather than made than that of George Armstrong Custer. Variously called Armstrong, Autie, Bo, Curly, Funny, Long Hair, and Yellow Hair, his meteoric rise to high command in the days of the old horse cavalry left most of his peers standing in the stable. Custer was one of the few figures favored by history to achieve legendary status in his own lifetime. Many of his accomplishments will likely never be equaled in modern times. Any story about the campaign that led to Custer's untimely end at the Little Bighorn would at best be incomplete without a glimpse at his beginnings and early career.

"My Boy Custer!"

Custer was born on December 5, 1839, in New Rumley, Ohio. He set his sights on becoming a soldier at an early age. He hit his mark at the age of eighteen, when Congressman John A. Bingham appointed him to the U.S. Military Academy at West Point. Custer began his military career with a thud, accumulating a record number of demerits and graduating last in his class in 1861. Only the outbreak of the

Civil War saved the brash and troublesome young man from certain expulsion from the army's prestigious academy. Seeking a return on its three-year investment in Custer, the government reluctantly commissioned him a second lieutenant in the Union Army.

George Armstrong Custer poses in his cadet uniform for this 1861 photograph. Despite his military aspirations, while attending the U.S. Military Academy at West Point Custer received numerous demerits and graduated last in his class.

A Boyish Prediction

"In June, 1857, I entered the Military Academy at West Point as a cadet," wrote George A. Custer, *"having received my appointment thereto through the kindness of the Hon. John W. Bingham, then representing in Congress the district in Ohio in which I was born, and in which I spent almost my entire boyhood."* Custer went on to describe how growing signs of a Southern secession from the Union affected life at the academy.

"I remember a conversation held at the [dining] table at which I sat during the winter of '60–'61. I was seated next to Cadet P. B. M. Young, a gallant young fellow from Georgia, a classmate of mine, . . . a major-general in the Confederate forces during the war. . . . The approaching war was as usual the subject of conversation in which we all participated. . . . Finally, in a half jocular half earnest manner, Young turned to me and delivered himself as follows: 'Custer, my boy, we're going to have war. It's no use talking: I can see it coming. All the [Senator John J.] Crittenden [of Kentucky] compromises that can be patched up won't avert it. Now let me prophesy what will happen to you and me. You will go home, and your abolition Governor will probably make you a colonel of a cavalry regiment. I will go down to Georgia, and ask Governor Brown to give me a cavalry regiment. And who knows but we may move against each other during the war. You will probably get the advantage over us in the first few engagements, as your side will be rich and powerful, while we will be poor and weak. Your regiment will be armed with the best of weapons, the sharpest of sabres; mine will have only shotguns and scythe blades; but for all that we'll get the best of the fight in the end, because we will fight for a principle, a cause, while you will fight only to perpetuate the abuse of power.' Lightly as we both regarded this boyish prediction, it was destined to be fulfilled in a remarkable degree. Early in the war I did apply, not to the abolition Governor of my native State, but to that of Michigan, for a cavalry regiment. I was refused, but afterward obtained the regiment I desired as part of my command. Young was chosen to lead one of the Georgia cavalry regiments. Both of us rose to higher commands, and confronted each other on the battlefield."

Custer (lying beside his dog) relaxes with other soldiers during the Civil War. The long war transformed the brash young lieutenant into a distinguished soldier and leader.

On July 21, 1861, fresh out of West Point three days earlier, Custer joined G Company, Second Cavalry, in the field outside Centerville, Virginia. Hours later, he met an armed enemy for the first time in the battle known as First Bull Run. Although the Confederate soldiers, led by Brigadier General Pierre G. T. Beauregard, routed their Union adversaries in that bloody engagement, Custer fought with gallantry and distinction. He exhibited the several qualities of leadership, courage, audacity, and swashbuckling recklessness that would soon become part and parcel of the Custer image.

Of his army's humiliating defeat, a disappointed Custer later wrote: "I little imagined when making my night ride from Washington on July 20th, that the night following would find me returning with a defeated and demoralized army." One of the last to leave the battle site, Custer marched his detail in an orderly retreat toward Washington, while other Union forces fled the scene in horror-stricken disarray. Boy bugler Joseph Fought recalled:

> The roads were jammed with people clamoring for news of the fight. But, though famished, exhausted, spent, Custer never let up, never slackened control. Then, when Arlington was reached and his company assigned to its camp, he snatched a few hours' sleep, beneath a tree, in a pouring rain, even while his name was being cited for bravery in the Capital.[39]

News of Custer's bravery soon reached the Washington office of the Honorable John A. Bingham. The congressional representative who had appointed Custer to West Point had lost track of his young appointee over the years. But, as Bingham reminisced:

> I heard of him after the First Battle of Bull Run. In the report of that miserable fiasco he was mentioned for bravery.

While in Washington, D.C., the famous Civil War–era photographer Mathew Brady took this portrait of Custer, then a general in the cavalry.

A leader was needed to re-form the troops, and take them over a bridge. Like Napoleon at Lodi young Custer sprang to the front—and was a hero.

I heard of his exploit with pride, and hunted several times for my boy, but unsuccessfully. Then one day a young soldier came to my room without the formality of sending a card.

Beautiful as Absalom with his yellow curls, he was out of breath, or had lost it from embarrassment. And he spoke with hesitation: "Mr. Bingham, I've been in my first battle. I tried hard to do my best. I felt I ought to report to you, for it's through you I got to West Point. I'm . . ."

I took his hand. "I know. You're my boy Custer!"[40]

Stepping Up

Always in action's forefront, Custer went on to participate in many of the war's major battles and campaigns: Antietam, Fredericksburg, Chancellorsville, Gettysburg, Yellow Tavern, Winchester, Fisher's Hill, and Five Forks.

In May 1862, during the Richmond Peninsula campaign (in which Major General George B. McClellan's Grand Army of the Potomac pursued Confederate general Joseph E. Johnston's overmatched Army of Northern Virginia), Custer was ordered to conduct a solitary, extremely hazardous reconnaissance to find a ford across the Chickahominy River. Custer forded the river safely and continued on to discover a Confederate outpost. Ordered before General McClellan upon his return, a soggy, mud-smeared Custer reported his findings with enthusiasm. McClellan later wrote about his first meeting with the young lieutenant:

Custer was simply a reckless, gallant boy, undeterred by fatigue, unconscious of fear; but his head was always clear in danger and he always brought me clear and intelligible reports of what he saw under the heaviest of fire. I became much attached to him.[41]

McClellan invited Custer to join his staff with the rank of captain. Custer accepted without hesitation and took his first upward step toward high command and military renown.

Boy General

Captain Custer suffered the first setback of his military career five months later. On November 7, 1862, President Abraham Lincoln dismissed General McClellan as head of the Grand Army of the Potomac. McClellan had failed to perform up to Lincoln's expectations. Worse, "Little Mac" had taken to criticizing the president's policies. Following McClellan's dismissal, Custer's rank reverted to first lieutenant of the Fifth U.S. Cavalry.

In the spring of 1863, after a long winter leave in Monroe, Michigan (where he began courting his future wife, Elizabeth Bacon), Custer joined the staff of Brigadier General Alfred Pleasonton, commander of a cavalry division. Pleasonton, himself averse to the hazards of sweeping sabers and flying shot, noticed at once that Custer seemed to thrive on danger. The general then began relying heavily on Custer to deliver messages to embattled field commanders. Pleasonton often empowered Custer to use his own judgment and issue his own orders to senior officers in the field. A strong bond developed between the general and his aide.

Pleasonton's growing trust and the impending Gettysburg campaign soon combined to speed Custer on his way to battlefield eminence. At Brandy Station, Virginia, on June 9, 1863, Custer rode in one of Pleasonton's mounted columns that spearheaded an attack against Confederate major general J. E. B. Stuart's famed cavalry division. The confrontation ended in a draw, but Custer again distinguished himself in what resulted in the largest purely cavalry battle of the war. Pleasonton's subsequent promotion to major general delighted his young aide: "Which makes me a captain again!"[42] wrote the elated Custer.

Eight days later, in a sharp clash at nearby Aldie, the First Maine Cavalry fell back before a fierce rebel surge. Custer helped rally the recoiling Maine troopers and led a spirited counterattack. A Michigan newspaper reported Custer's action:

> Outstripping his men in pursuit of the enemy, one of them [the enemy] turned, fired, but missed, his revolver being knocked by a sword blow that sent the rider toppling to the ground. Another enemy trooper tore alongside, but Custer, giving his horse a sudden check, let the man go shooting by. Then face to face they fought it out, gray going down before the blue. . . .
>
> Gen. [Joseph] Hooker [then commanding the Grand Army of the Potomac] asserts that we have not a more gallant man [than Custer] in the field, and that wherever there is a daring expedition or hard fighting to be done, he is always among the foremost.[43]

On Friday evening, June 26, 1863, while temporarily based at Camp Frederick in west-central Maryland, Captain G. A.

Custer received an envelope from Washington. After opening it to the hurrahs of his fellow officers, he dashed off a letter to his dear Elizabeth:

> Be the first at home to hear of my good fortune. Believe it or not, I have been promoted to a *Brigadier-General!* I certainly have a great cause to rejoice. I am the youngest Gen'l in the U.S. Army by over two years—in itself something to be proud of. My appointment dates from the 20th of June. I owe it all to Gen'l Pleasonton. He has been more like a father to me than a Gen'l.[44]

The June 27, 1863, edition of the New York *Herald* hailed Custer as "the Boy General with the Golden Locks."[45] Custer was all of twenty-three years old when he earned the highly controversial and nearly unheard-of brevet promotion to brigadier general of volunteers. (A brevet rank is one higher than that for which a military officer receives pay; a commission in the volunteers was comparable to a reserve appointment in today's army.) The following year, the "boy general" married Elizabeth Bacon, the beautiful love of his life.

The Stuff of Legends

The new brigadier general took command of the Second Brigade, Third Cavalry Division. Because all four of its regiments (the First, Fifth, Sixth, and Seventh) were drawn from Michigan, Custer's new command was known simply as the Michigan (or Wolverine) Brigade. "When I assumed command," Custer wrote later, "few if any of the men . . . had even heard a hostile shot fired, their discipline lax and organization incom-

plete."[46] Their combat training began less than a week later on the rolling hills three miles east of Gettysburg, Pennsylvania.

On July 3, 1863, Custer led five hundred First Michigan Wolverines against more than two thousand of Jeb Stuart's crack "Invincibles"—the cream of General Robert E. Lee's cavalry. Custer galloped to the front of his regiment, waved his saber, and before disappearing in a swarm of on-rushing rebels, shouted, "Come on, you Wolverines!"[47] Custer's Michiganders streaked after their dauntless leader in a screaming, snarling, slashing, stabbing, shooting cavalry charge. Under Custer's intrepid leadership, the Wolverines turned

Custer and his longtime sweetheart, Elizabeth Bacon, were married shortly after he was promoted to brigadier general.

"A Fair, Square Fight"

In early May 1864, General Philip H. Sheridan summoned his generals and said, "We are going out to fight Stuart's Cavalry. . . . We will give him a fair, square fight. . . . I shall expect nothing but success." In his memoirs, Sheridan went on to write:

"Our move would be a challenge to Stuart for a cavalry duel, behind Lee's lines, in his own country. [The great cavalry clash took place at a crossroads in Virginia called Yellow Tavern on May 11, 1864.]

Early on May 9th the expedition started toward Fredericksburg. . . . About dark [Brigadier General Wesley] Merritt's Division crossed the North Anna. . . . Custer's Brigade proceeded on to Beaver Dam Station. . . . He met a small force of the enemy, but this he speedily drove off, recapturing from it about four hundred Union prisoners being taken to Richmond. . . . He destroyed the station, two locomotives, three trains of cars, ninety wagons, from eight to ten miles of railroad and telegraph lines . . . munitions, rations, supplies intended for Lee's army. . . .

By forced marches General Stuart reached Yellow Tavern on the 11th. The enemy, desperate but confident, poured a heavy fire from his line and from a battery [of artillery].

. . . Gibbs' and Devin's brigades, however, held fast, while Custer, supported by Chapman's Brigade, attacked the enemy's left and battery in a mounted charge. . . .

Custer's charge was brilliantly executed. Beginning at a walk he increased this to a trot, then, at full speed, rushed on the enemy. . . .

After Custer's charge the Confederate Cavalry was badly broken up. . . . The engagement ended by giving us complete control of the road to Richmond."

back the rebels in a stunning victory. By battle's end, Brigadier General George A. Custer had earned the undying loyalty and respect of his soldiers.

Of Custer, one of his troopers wrote: "He is a glorious fellow, full of energy, quick to plan and bold to execute, and with us he has never failed in any attempt he has yet made."[48]

A Fifth Michigan private witnessed Custer in close combat and wrote later that he saw Custer "plunge his saber into the belly of a rebel who was trying to kill him. You can guess how bravely soldiers fight for such a general."[49]

A Yankee captain in the Third Cavalry Division wrote: "With Custer as leader we are all heroes and hankering for a fight."[50]

After watching Custer direct a skirmish, one of his aides wrote: "Through all that sharp and heavy firing the General gave his orders as though conducting a parade or review, so cool and indifferent that he inspired us all with something of his coolness and courage."[51] Of such stuff are legends born.

Luck and Politics

Custer, as people often do when rising rapidly to fame and gain, accumulated many friends and at least as many enemies along his ascending career path. While reaping praise from friends for his courage, daring, and successes, he garnered an equal amount of criticism from jealous competitors. Those who felt less kindly to the youthful phenomenon attributed his impressive accomplishments more to luck than ability. As a means of explaining away Custer's battlefield successes, "Custer's Luck" became a stock phrase in the vocabulary of his detractors.

Early in 1864, while Custer continued to distinguish himself on the battlefield, he learned from friendly contacts that unnamed enemies in Washington were trying to undermine his appointment as brevet brigadier general in the regular army. Unable to fault his service record, Custer's detractors tried to discredit his politics, accusing him of trying to sabotage the administration's war policies—including President Abraham Lincoln's controversial Emancipation Proclamation.

In a frantic effort to clear himself of false charges and save his commission, Custer wrote an eight-page letter to Michigan senator Jacob M. Howard, part of which follows:

> The President . . . as Commander in Chief of the Army and as my Superior officer Cannot issue any decree or order which will not receive my unqualified *support*. . . . But I do *not* stop here. . . . All his acts, proclamations and decisions embraced in his war policy have received not only my support, but my most hearty, earnest and cordial *approval*. . . . My friends . . . *can* testify that I have insisted that so long as a single slave was held in bondage, I for *one*, was opposed to peace on any terms, and to show that my acts agree with my words I can boast of having liberated more slaves from their Masters than any other General in this Army. . . . I would *offer* no compromise except that which is offered at the point of the bayonet.[52]

Confirmation of his appointment passed through Congress in record time. Moreover, Ohio senator Ben Wade suggested raising Custer to major general "as soon as a vacancy occurs."[53]

A Fine Tribute

That vacancy occurred while Custer was serving under Major General Philip H. "Little Phil" Sheridan, commander of the forty-thousand-man Army of the Shenandoah. On September 30, 1864, after a decisive Union victory in the Battle of Winchester, in Virginia, Sheridan handed Custer command of the Third Cavalry Division in recognition of Custer's role in a pivotal cavalry charge. Sheridan made no secret of his respect for his young subordinate. "Custer is the ablest man in the Cavalry Corps,"[54] he declared.

Ten days later, under Custer's dynamic leadership, the Third Cavalry slammed through the left flank of Lieutenant General Jubal A. Early's Confederate army at Cedar Creek, Virginia, capturing forty-five cannons and droves of prisoners. This time, Little Phil rewarded Custer with the brevet rank of major general. On March 2, 1865, Custer extended his thanks to Sheridan by smashing the remnants of Early's army at Waynesboro, Virginia.

With the Shenandoah Valley cleared and the war drawing to a close, General Sheridan moved his forces eastward to join General Grant. Meanwhile, General Lee abandoned Richmond and fled west to spare his troops from starvation and encirclement by Union forces. Sheridan gave chase to Lee's fleeing forces with four cavalry divisions. Custer's Third Cavalry led the pursuit.

At dusk on April 8, Custer came under heavy fire from thirty guns of Lee's reserve artillery at Appomattox Station, in Virginia. Custer led several cavalry sweeps against the rebel cannons. An enlisted man of the Second Ohio Cavalry reported: "We expected Custer would be killed every time, but he was not scratched, tho he had a horse or two killed under him. He really appeared to lead a charmed life."[55] By nightfall, twenty-four of the thirty rebel guns belonged to Custer.

The next day, April 9, 1865, Custer received the first Confederate flag of truce.

General Lee surrendered to General Grant in the parlor of the Wilmer McLean house several hours later. General Sheridan bought the table on which the surrender documents had been drafted and shipped it to Elizabeth Custer. Little Phil's accompanying note said:

> I respectfully present to you the small writing-table on which the conditions for the surrender of the Confederate Army of Northern Virginia were written by Lt. General Grant—and permit me to say, Madam, that there is scarcely an individual in our service who has contributed more to bring this about than your very gallant husband.[56]

Few soldiers have received any finer tribute; few soldiers have been so deserving.

The Postwar Years

A brevet major general and chief of cavalry by war's end, Custer was caught in a personnel cutback that forced a massive reduction of rank within the army's officer corps. He reverted to his earlier rank of captain but was promoted soon after to lieutenant colonel and given command of the newly formed Seventh Cavalry Regiment at Fort Riley, Kansas, in 1867. Custer relished the opportunity for renewed action, donning buckskins for his frontier assignment and playing the role of Indian fighter as an actor plays Hamlet.

An entry in Elizabeth's diary revealed her husband's delight with his new life: "Autie scarcely leaves the garrison behind him, where he is bound by chains of form and ceremony, when he becomes the

Letter of Appreciation

On the evening of April 9, 1865, after Generals Grant and Lee had reached a peace accord at Appomattox, sleep would not come to Major General George A. Custer until he had written the following letter to the soldiers of the Third Cavalry Division.

"The record established by your indomitable courage is unparalleled in the annals of war. Your prowess has won for you even the respect and admiration of your enemies. During the past six months, although in most instances confronted by superior numbers, you have captured from the enemy in open battle, one hundred and eleven pieces of field artillery, sixty-five battle-flags, and upwards of ten thousand prisoners, including seven general officers. Within the past ten days, and included in the above, you have captured forty-six pieces of field artillery, and thirty-seven battle-flags. You have never lost a gun, never lost a color, and have never been defeated; and notwithstanding the numerous engagements in which you have borne a prominent part, including those memorable battles of the Shenandoah, you have captured every piece of artillery which the enemy has dared to open upon you. The near approach of peace renders it improbable that you will again be called upon to undergo the fatigues of the toilsome march or the exposure of the battlefield, but should the assistance of keen blades, wielded by sturdy arms, be required to hasten the coming of that glorious peace for which we have been so long contending, the General commanding is proudly confident that, in the future, as in the past, every demand will be met with a hearty and willing response. . . .

And now, speaking for myself alone, when the war is ended and the task of the historian begins—when those deeds of daring which have rendered the name and fame of the Third Cavalry Division imperishable, are inscribed upon the bright pages of our country's history, I only ask that my name may be written as that of the Commander of the Third Cavalry Division."

wildest and most frolicsome of light-hearted boys. His horse and he are one."[57]

After serving as a field commander under General Winfield Scott Hancock from April through July 1867, young "Yellow Hair" (as many Indians called Custer) ran afoul of military justice for desertion (he left camp without leave to visit his wife) and for overmarching his men and treating deserters too harshly. A court-martial convicted him on both counts and suspended him from rank and pay for a year. General Sheridan intervened on Custer's behalf, however, and the army reinstated Custer in time for him to command the Seventh Cavalry in Sheridan's winter campaign of 1868.

Custer's subsequent destruction of Black Kettle's village on the Washita River excited a storm of controversy. Critics claimed that Custer had directed the willful slaughter of peaceful Indians, mostly women and children. The army defended the attack, maintaining that no matter how much Black Kettle wanted peace, his camp yielded abundant evidence that his warriors were the ones responsible for terrorizing white settlements in Kansas. Also, the Indians had been holding four white captives, two of whom they killed during Custer's attack.

In the spring of 1869, with the Indian problem seemingly settled, at least temporarily, the army withdrew the Seventh Cavalry from the frontier and reassigned it to garrison duty at Fort Leavenworth, Kansas. Custer next drew a two-year assignment in March 1871 as commandant of a two-company post at Elizabethtown, Kentucky. The Custers left the plains, which, as Elizabeth wrote, had become "dear to us, because of the happy hours spent there."[58]

During 1869–1872, the army scattered the companies of the Seventh Cavalry in various posts for a variety of reasons, few of which bore significantly on the drama that started unfolding in 1873. An avid and prolific writer, Custer took advantage of the more leisurely garrison lifestyle to write a series of articles for the magazine *Galaxy*, starting in January 1872 and ending in October 1874. These articles, collectively

In 1867 Custer was assigned to Fort Riley, Kansas, and given command of the Seventh Cavalry. Custer enthusiastically accepted the move to the frontier outpost, trading in his army uniform for a pair of buckskins.

entitled "My Life on the Plains" (eventually reprinted in book form), recounted his experiences on the western frontier and added to his romantic image as an Indian-fighter.

Dakota Territory

In the spring of 1873, representatives of the Northern Pacific Railroad asked the government to protect its survey team from hostile Indian attacks west of the Missouri River. Custer was ordered to the Dakota Territory. Elizabeth, who had enjoyed two years of comfort and security in Kentucky, went with him. One of her diary entries reflected her fears for the future:

> This removal to Dakota means to Autie a reunion with his [regiment] and summer campaigns against Indians; to me it means months of loneliness, anxiety and terror. But I shall honor my father's dying words: "Follow him everywhere. It is your Destiny to make him happy."[59]

Elizabeth, come what might, shared her husband's sense of destiny.

Reunited for the first time since Washita, Custer and the Seventh Cavalry escorted the surveyors into the Dakota Territory on the Yellowstone Expedition,

Custer and wife, Elizabeth, dine in a tent while stationed in Kansas in 1869. A devoted wife, Elizabeth accompanied her husband despite the dangers of the frontier.

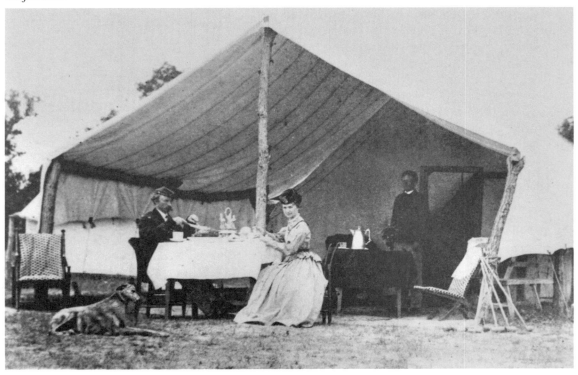

A bearded Custer sits among his scouts during the 1873 Yellowstone Expedition. The campaign explored some 935 miles of Dakota Territory and gave Custer's Seventh Cavalry opportunities to engage Indians in combat.

covering 935 miles in sixty-six days. Skirmishes with Indian war parties that summer provided the cavalrymen with Indian-fighting experience and Custer with added material for his ongoing literary endeavors.

In September 1873, Custer assumed command of Fort Abraham Lincoln, Dakota Territory. During the following summer, Custer and the Seventh Cavalry accompanied the Black Hills Expedition into uncharted Indian country, supposedly to map out possible routes between Fort Lincoln and Fort Laramie. While blazing the so-called Thieves' Trail across lands ceded to the Indians, the expedition found ore samples that confirmed earlier rumors of gold in the area. From Fort Lincoln, Custer informed the War Department that insufficient information had been obtained "to warrant an immense influx of gold hunters into that region in advance of a more thorough and deliberate examination."[60]

Custer might just as well have whispered his message in the wind. When

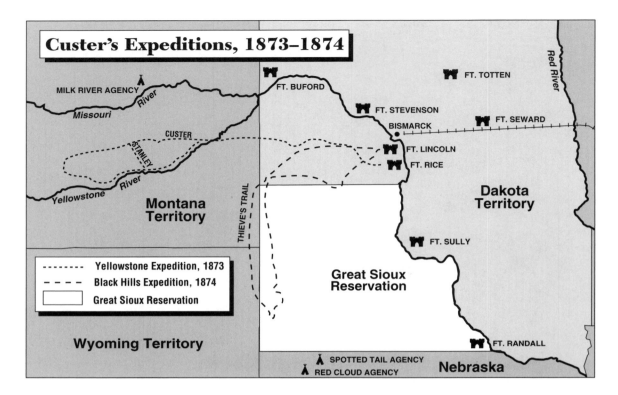

Custer's Expeditions, 1873–1874

MILK RIVER AGENCY

Missouri River

CUSTER

STANLEY

Yellowstone River

Montana Territory

FT. BUFORD

FT. TOTTEN

Red River

FT. STEVENSON

BISMARCK

FT. SEWARD

FT. LINCOLN

FT. RICE

Dakota Territory

THIEVE'S TRAIL

FT. SULLY

Great Sioux Reservation

- - - - - - Yellowstone Expedition, 1873
- - - - Black Hills Expedition, 1874
□ Great Sioux Reservation

Wyoming Territory

FT. RANDALL

SPOTTED TAIL AGENCY
RED CLOUD AGENCY

Nebraska

word of his message confirming gold reached the ears of a citizenry still suffering from the throes of postwar depression, gold seekers commenced a "grand rush"[61] into Dakota Territory.

The army tried to bar all white people from entering the Black Hills. General Sheridan warned miners and prospectors to stay out of the area, declaring that treaty agreements had exempted any white settlement in that country. Nevertheless, several parties of gold miners slipped through to the diggings and returned with exaggerated claims of the riches to be found there. Thousands of gold seekers followed the Thieves' Trail into the Black Hills within the next year. The Indians complained about the trespassing whites but remained peaceful. But not for long.

3 Sitting Bull: Soldiers Falling into Camp

Unable to stem the flow of prospectors into the Black Hills, the government tried instead to buy the coveted land from the Indians, but they refused to sell. Those Indians opposed to the sale threatened to kill anyone who might be tempted to sign a bill of sale. The opposition leader was a tawny, broad-shouldered Hunkpapa Sioux with a flint-eyed stare, called Sitting Bull.

Chief of the Hunkpapas, medicine man, and spiritual leader whose revered wisdom influenced the entire Sioux Nation, Sitting Bull told the agency Indians: "You are fools to make yourselves slaves to a piece of fat bacon, some hard-tack, and a little sugar and coffee."[62] Angered and saddened by what he saw as the government's betrayal of his people, Sitting Bull vowed to fight the white invaders in defense of Indian homelands and families:

> We have been deceived by the white people. The Black Hills country was set aside for us by the Government. It was ours by solemn agreement, and we made the country our home. Our homes in the Black Hills were invaded when gold was discovered there. Now, the Indian must raise his arm to protect his women, his children, his

Sitting Bull, the revered leader of the Hunkpapa Sioux, addresses a meeting of braves. Sitting Bull vehemently denounced the sale of Indian lands to the U.S. government.

home; and if the Government lets loose an army upon us to kill without mercy, we shall fight as brave men fight. We shall meet our enemies and honorably defeat them, or we shall all of us die in disgrace.[63]

General George A. Custer, one of those whom the government would soon "let loose" upon the Indians, empathized with their plight. "I can't say I blame the poor savages," he said, "but apparently there is no stopping progress and civilization, undesirable though they may be to the romantic spirit."[64]

Grant's Decision

Following the Treaty of Laramie in 1868, most of the Northern Plains Indians—a few northern Cheyennes, Arapahos, and Eastern Sioux, but mostly the Teton (or Western) Sioux: Oglalas, Hunkpapas, Brulé, Miniconjou, Sans Arc, and Black-

foot—had retired to live peacefully on the Great Sioux Reservation. Except for occasional minor conflicts between *nontreaties* (the government's term for Indians who opted to live independently off the reservation) and settlers and travelers in the unceded territory, the Indians pretty much kept the peace until the mid-1870s. With the coming of the railroad and the discovery of gold in the Black Hills, the Sioux Wars became at once foreseeable and inevitable.

While peace prevailed, some three thousand nontreaties—about four hundred Cheyennes and a mixed complement of Teton Sioux—would congregate in the unceded territory during the summer for buffalo hunts. But when the white man's rails cut through vital grazing lands (as they were allowed to do by treaty), the once plentiful buffalo herds began to diminish rapidly. White hunters came to hasten the buffalo's demise. With the discovery of gold in the Black Hills, the white man's rush for riches ran roughshod over the Indians' sovereign rights within the

Buffalo are slaughtered as a locomotive blazes through their grazing lands. The railroad, as well as white hunters, hastened the demise of the buffalo.

Ruthless Indians terrorize a wagon train and gamble for possession of the female captive in this fanciful drawing. Illustrations like this one were created to turn the American public against the "savages."

Great Sioux Reservation. Hostile encounters between Indians and whites increased. Most of the violence was precipitated by Indian attempts to bar gold seekers and other white intruders from ceded land and unceded territory alike.

President Ulysses S. Grant's government in Washington found itself caught between two irreconcilable responsibilities as unyielding as flint and steel: a just administration of Indian rights on the one hand; and the pacification of a white citizenry clamoring for riches and Manifest Destiny on the other. Grant had a choice between sending the army against trespassing whites to enforce the law or against law-abiding Indians to seize and claim the disputed land as spoils of war.

On November 3, 1875, at a secret White House meeting, President Grant announced to a few handpicked cabinet members and army generals—General

Philip H. Sheridan most prominent among them—that he had decided to make war.

The Indian Problem

President Grant's decision and the subsequent mobilization of troops were kept secret while the government waged a campaign of propaganda and disinformation against the Indians. Washington hoped by such deception to convince the public that the war, when it came, came as a result of increasing acts of Indian violence. In other words, responsibility for the upcoming war would lie not with the conniving government but with the "renegade" Indians.

Not surprisingly, President Grant directed General Sheridan, then commanding the Military Division of the Missouri, and key military members present at the White House meeting to prepare for a military campaign against the Indians. Sheridan immediately started planning a winter campaign similar to those that had earlier proven successful against Indians of the southern plains.

On that same day, in a letter to President Grant, Indian Bureau inspector Erwin C. Watkins reported innumerable instances of Indian misconduct (curiously vague as to time and date of the alleged violations). Watkins's report was obviously intended to clear the way for military action against the Sioux:

> In my judgement, one thousand men under the command of an experienced officer, sent into their country in the winter, when the Indians are nearly always in camp, and at which season of the year they are the most helpless, would be amply sufficient for their capture or punishment. . . .
>
> The true policy in my judgement, is to send troops against them in the winter, the sooner the better, and *whip* them into subjection. They richly merit the punishment for their incessant warfare on friendly tribes [principally the Crows], their continuous thieving, and their numerous murders of white settlers and their families, or white men found unarmed.
>
> The Government owes it, too, to these friendly tribes, in fulfillment of treaty stipulations. It owes it to the agents and employees, whom it has sent to labor among the Indians at remote and almost inaccessible places, beyond reach in time to save. It owes it to the frontier settlers who have, with their families, braved the dangers and hardships incident to frontier life. It owes it to civilization and the common cause of humanity.[65]

Coincidentally, or otherwise, General Phil Sheridan's plan called for a winter campaign against the Indians. Little Phil stood eager, with one thousand soldiers and whip in hand, to prosecute a permanent solution to the "Indian problem."

Powder River

In a December 3 letter to Secretary of War William W. Belnap, with Washington's propaganda and disinformation campaign against the Indians well underway, Secretary of the Interior Zachariah Chandler wrote:

> I have the honor to inform you that I have this day directed the Commissioner of Indian Affairs to notify said [nontreaty] Indians that they must remove to a reservation before the 31st of January next; that if they neglect or refuse so to move, they will be reported to the War Department as hostile Indians and that a military force will be sent to compel them to obey the orders of the Indian Office.[66]

Three days later, the government then dropped all pretext of fair dealing with the Indians. Indian Commissioner Edward P. Smith issued instructions to his agents at Red Cloud, Spotted Tail, Standing Rock, Cheyenne River, Fort Peck, Lower Brulé, Crow Creek, and Devil's Lake Agencies to inform Sitting Bull and other hostile chiefs to report to their agencies by

No Place to Hide

In winter of 1876, severe weather conditions and logistical problems forced Lieutenant General Philip H. Sheridan to abandon his planned three-column offensive against the Indians. Instead, he settled for Brigadier General George Crook's one-column expedition out of Fort Fetterman, Wyoming. On February 22, 1876, after rumors of Crook's expedition began circulating in Cheyenne, Robert E. Strahorn, a journalist with the Denver Rocky Mountain News, *interviewed the general about his impending campaign. An excerpt from that interview follows.*

"As early as last December an order was issued by proper authorities, the disobeyance of which by the Indians was the direct cause of this campaign. The order was to the effect that all the tribes of the Sioux then off their reservations should immediately repair thereto, and that if they failed to obey by the 31st of January, they would be considered enemies and thoroughly chastised.

Lying north and northwest of Fort Fetterman is a vast scope of country known as the "unceded lands," to which the Indians have no right or title [not true], but in which the most warlike of them have sought refuge, rest, and succor ever since the abandonment of that region by the military and settlers during the massacre of 1866. Since that date, those bands of Sioux who bid defiance to our attempts at reconciliation, have marauded north, south, and east of this, their natural stronghold. . . . These tribes were included in the order referred to above; but not only have they treated the order with supreme contempt they have made redoubled efforts in the way of replenishing their supplies of arms and ammunition, etc. . . .

The reason[s] given for the hasty and quiet manner in which [General Crook] has thus so far proceeded, are simply, first, that he is determined to strike a blow at once which will demoralize the savages from the start; second, that a winter campaign, although terribly arduous in that region, will have thrice the terror of one two months later; third, because everything points to a general Indian war in the section adjacent to the Black Hills, even in the advance of the advent of spring, and to make the small force at his command adequate to the demands of next summer's task, Gen. Crook sees the prime necessity of . . . showing . . . that the Black Hills and Powder River regions are not to be made the hiding place of the whole Sioux nation, in case of its general defeat."

January 31, 1876, or be hunted and killed as hostiles. Predictably, none of the "hostiles" reported to the reservation by the declared deadline.

On March 1, 1876, Brigadier General George Crook left Fort Fetterman, Wyoming, with a column of nine hundred men and moved north. Sheridan planned to attack the Indians with three columns converging from three directions. The other two columns were to organize in the Department of Dakota, Brigadier General Alfred H. Terry commanding, with Colonel John Gibbon trekking east from bases in western Montana, and Lieutenant Colonel George A. Custer marching west from Fort Abraham Lincoln.

Sheridan's campaign faltered when put into practice, however, foiled by heavy snows and brutally cold conditions on the plains. Of the Dakota contingents, only

Gibbon's column marched. Custer's departure was postponed when the snows blocked rail passage and delayed delivery of his supplies. Meanwhile, Crook's column found a trail leading to a village of Oglalas and Cheyennes beside the Powder River.

On March 17, after three weeks of battling snow and icy winds, Crook sent Colonel Joseph J. Reynolds and a detachment of three hundred cavalry troops to attack the village of 105 lodges. Reynolds took the Indians by surprise, forcing them to flee to bluffs bordering the river. One of Reynolds's squadrons proceeded to raze the village, while a second squadron concentrated on seizing the Indian pony herd. The troopers had barely begun their work when the Oglalas, led by He Dog, and the Cheyennes, under Old Bear, mounted a vigorous counterattack.

U.S. soldiers approach Fort Fetterman, headquarters of General Crook, in this 1876 engraving. On March 1, 1876, Crook and his troops left the fort, embarking on their frigid march north.

With his supplies quickly depleted, General Crook abandoned the winter campaign and returned to Fort Fetterman. When spring finally arrived, Crook and his forces renewed their efforts to vanquish the Indians.

Colonel Reynolds quickly ordered a withdrawal and the Indians regained their village and recaptured most of their ponies. Reynolds, in his hasty flight, left behind the bodies of several dead troopers. Worse, he abandoned a wounded trooper, Private Lorenzo Ayers, of M Company, Third Cavalry, sacrificing the unfortunate soldier to the inevitable savagery of the Indians. (The Indians cut Ayers apart limb from limb.) When Reynolds rejoined Crook's main column, a disgusted Crook, with his supplies running low, decided to return to Fort Fetterman.

Back at the fort, Crook promptly brought charges against Reynolds for what was politely termed "mismanagement" of both the attack and retreat at Powder River. Reynolds pled his case to General Sheridan. "General," Reynolds protested, "these winter campaigns in these latitudes should be prohibited. . . . The month of March has told on me more than any five years of my life."[67] A compassionate Sheridan attributed Reynolds's poor performance to the weather and temporarily set aside the charges.

Reynolds's aborted attack at Powder River won dubious honor as one of the U.S. Cavalry's sorriest showings ever. Moreover, it demonstrated to the Indians that the army intended to enforce Grant's ultimatum, causing them to band together in a larger, stronger fighting force under the inspired leadership of Crazy Horse and Sitting Bull.

General Terry, under the circumstances, ordered Gibbon's column to set up camp on the Yellowstone River. The winter campaign then dragged on until it became a spring—and ultimately a summer—campaign.

Sitting Bull's Vision

On May 17, 1876, General Sheridan launched a spring version of what had begun as his winter campaign. General Terry himself led a force of 925 infantry and cavalry troops from the east (including Custer and the Seventh Cavalry). At about the same time, Gibbon resumed his eastward march along the Yellowstone River with a mixed cavalry and infantry force of 450. Crook headed north again, on May 29, with a mounted force (including infantrymen) of more than a thousand men. Because the location of the

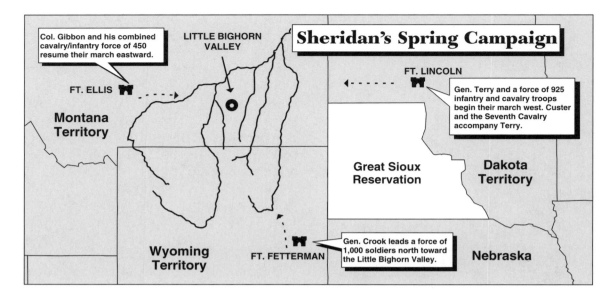

Col. Gibbon and his combined cavalry/infantry force of 450 resume their march eastward.

LITTLE BIGHORN VALLEY

Sheridan's Spring Campaign

FT. LINCOLN

Gen. Terry and a force of 925 infantry and cavalry troops begin their march west. Custer and the Seventh Cavalry accompany Terry.

FT. ELLIS

Montana Territory

Great Sioux Reservation

Dakota Territory

Wyoming Territory

FT. FETTERMAN

Gen. Crook leads a force of 1,000 soldiers north toward the Little Bighorn Valley.

Nebraska

Indians was unknown and "there would be no way of telling how long they would stay in any one place, even if it were known,"[68] General Sheridan made no attempt to coordinate the movements of the three columns.

On the day of Crook's departure, Sheridan summed up his view of the developing situation to General Sherman. Little Phil explained that he had

> given no instructions to Generals Crook or Terry, preferring that they should do the best they can under the circumstances and under what they may develop, as I think it would be unwise to make any combinations in such country as they will have to operate in. As hostile Indians in any great numbers can not keep the field as a body for a week, or at most ten days, I therefore consider—and so do Terry and Crook—that each column will be able to take care of itself and of chastising the Indians should it have the opportunity.[69]

Sheridan figured that his three converging columns would eventually steer the Indians toward the Yellowstone River and trap them somewhere in the vicinity of the Little Bighorn Valley. His strategy was not without merit. The Indians, once united and strengthened under Crazy Horse and Sitting Bull, had begun immediately working their way westward toward the Yellowstone River.

The incident at Powder River convinced the Indians that the soldiers had come not to protect settlers and the railroad but to kill Indians. The free-roaming Indians were then drawn naturally toward Sitting Bull. A Cheyenne called Wooden Leg explained why:

> He had come now into admiration by all Indians as a man whose medicine was good—that is, as a man having a kind heart and good judgment as to the best course of conduct. He was considered as being altogether brave, but peaceable. He was strong in religion—the Indian religion. He made

Wakantanka Speaks to Sitting Bull

Sitting Bull, or Tatanka-Iyotanka in the language of the Lakotas, considered himself predestined to become a holy man, or wichasha wakan. *During his first interview with a reporter, in which the interpreter undoubtedly substituted "God" for "Wakantanka," Sitting Bull said:*

"I was still in my mother's insides when I began to study all about my people. God (waving his hand to express a great protecting Genius) gave me the power to see out of the womb. I studied there, in the womb, about many things. I studied about the smallpox, that was killing my people—the great sickness that was killing the women and children. I was so interested that I turned over on my side. The God Almighty must have told me at that time (and here Sitting Bull unconsciously revealed his secret) that I would be the man to be the judge of all the other Indians—a big man, to decide for them in all their ways.

'And you have since decided for them?' the reporter asked.

'I speak. It is enough,' Sitting Bull replied."

By nature, wichasha wakan *dreamed sacred dreams and sometimes saw visions of great spiritual significance. Sitting Bull's most famous vision came to him early in June 1876.*

After dancing for a day and a half in the ceremony known as wiwanyag wachipi, *or the Sun Dance, Sitting Bull fell into a trance. When he finally regained his senses, he spoke softly to his cousin Black Moon, who rose and addressed the thousands of Sioux and Cheyennes in attendance:*

"Sitting Bull wishes to announce that he just heard a voice from above saying, 'I give you these because they have no ears.' He looked up and saw soldiers [with no ears because they would not listen] and some Indians on horseback coming down like grasshoppers, with their heads down and their hats falling off. They were falling right into our camp."

Soon thereafter it came to pass that many soldiers "fell" into Sitting Bull's camp at the Little Bighorn—never to rise again.

A young brave participates in the sacred Sun Dance. It was during this religious ceremony that Sitting Bull had a vision of soldiers "falling" into his camp along the Rosebud Creek.

medicine many times. He prayed and fasted and whipped his flesh into submission to the will of the Great Medicine [Supreme Entity or Power]. So, in attaching ourselves to the Uncpapas we other tribes were not moved by a desire to fight. They had not invited us. They simply welcomed us. We supposed that the combined camps would frighten off the soldiers. We hoped thus to be freed from their annoyance.[70]

By mid-June, Sitting Bull's camp, then located along Rosebud Creek in Montana, had grown to some 460 lodges and about three thousand people, including about eight hundred warriors. It was there that Sitting Bull held a religious ceremony known to Lakotas as *wiwanyag wachipi*, or dance looking at the sun (now called the Sun Dance). After the ceremony, Sitting Bull told his followers of having seen a great vision: one of many, many soldiers "falling right into our camp."[71]

4 Last Farewell: On to the Little Bighorn

Despite Indian pleas to be left alone to hunt buffalo and live off the land, the soldiers would not listen. As Sitting Bull's vision clearly showed, they had no ears with which to hear. They were coming anyway. Because the vision showed some Indians upside down, as well as many, many soldiers, some Indians would die in the fighting. But *all* of the soldiers would die. Sitting Bull's followers took courage from

Crazy Horse, the respected war leader of the Lakota, would lead a force of warriors to battle General Crook and his soldiers.

this vision of a great Indian victory and began preparing for the battle soon to come.

He Dog's and Old Bear's success in driving off the soldiers of Three Stars—as the Indians called General Crook—at the Powder River had inspired new confidence in Indian hearts. They began to believe themselves capable of defeating the soldiers at times and places of Indian choosing. Then many reservation Indians started arriving in Sitting Bull's camp for the spring and summer hunting seasons. The Indians' newfound confidence rose steadily in proportion to their swelling ranks. By mid-June, the Indians were spoiling for a fight.

Three Stars and his Wyoming column intended to oblige them.

Crazy Horse Rides

On the night of June 16, 1876, Lakota scouts rode into the camp of Sitting Bull and Crazy Horse. They brought news of Three Stars and many soldiers moving north from Goose Creek (near present-day Sheridan, Wyoming) and heading toward Rosebud Creek, about a night's ride away. Many Crows and Shoshones, longtime enemies of the Lakotas and Cheyennes, rode with Three Stars. The Indians held council in the main lodge and debated what to do. Most of the young braves wanted to ride at once against Three Stars. Many elder warriors advised caution and wanted to wait. After much haggling back and forth, the great Lakota war leader Crazy Horse stepped forward and said:

> My relatives, the bluecoat soldiers are different from us. That we know. They fight, but I think they are not warriors. They fight because it is their work. They are paid to do so. The Lakota warrior fights to protect his people, his family, and the good ways of the peo-ple. [He paused while the others present murmured their agreement.] It is time to put an end to the white man in our land. It is time to finish this thing. I will ride against Three Stars. Those who wish can come with me.[72]

About 750 young warriors stood forth to ride with Crazy Horse. They prepared themselves quickly for battle, donning war paint and good medicine charms, gathering up bows and full quivers, lances, rifles, war clubs, and the like, and selecting their best ponies. Leaving "those with many battles"[73] behind to protect the camp,

General Crook's army crosses the west fork of Goose Creek the day before the Battle of the Rosebud.

Wonderful Medicines

On the eve of his confrontation with General George Crook's Wyoming column, Crazy Horse led his eager warriors on a hard overnight ride south, across the Wolf Mountains and into the valley of the Rosebud. Crazy Horse and about 750 warriors arrived at the battle site at daybreak. Assembling behind a sheltering ridge, they paused to stretch their legs and nourish themselves, then completed their preparations for battle, which they had begun earlier in camp. John Stands in Timber, a grandson of two Sitting Bull followers, described how the warriors prepared for the Battle of the Rosebud.

"Many had ceremonies to perform and ornaments to put on before they went into war, and they knew it would not be long. So the chiefs gave the order and the warriors howled like wolves to answer them, and scattered here and there to begin picking out their shields and warbonnets and other things they used. Not too many had warbonnets though. More used mounted birds or animals and different kinds of charms.

There were many ways to perform ceremonies on the body. The warriors depended on being protected by the power that came from them. They could ride close to the soldiers and not be harmed. Some were wonderful medicines, like the mounted hawk of Brave Wolf's that he was given after fasting at Bear Butte. He would tie it on the back lock of his hair and ride into a fight whistling with a bone whistle. Sometimes on a charge the bird came to life and whistled too, when they came close to the enemy in hand-to-hand fighting. Many mentioned that bird. On the other hand, a man without power of some kind did not go in close that way. He did not dare."

While the warriors completed their last preparations, Crazy Horse and his war leaders climbed to the crest of the ridge and looked down at the shallow valley of the Rosebud. Because pine-covered ridges and deep crevices obscured their view of the soldiers' camp, Crazy Horse sent out scouts on horses for a better look.

The scouts ran into a party of Crow scouts on the opposite ridge. A Crow fired a single shot. More shots followed. Crazy Horse's eager warriors heard the gunfire and raced over the crest and into the valley of the Rosebud.

It was time to test their wonderful medicines.

Crazy Horse and his warriors rode out into the night and headed south toward Rosebud Creek.

"Death Is Not the Enemy!"

On June 17, Crook's soldiers answered reveille at 4:00 A.M. and resumed their northward march at 6:00 A.M. Two hours later, Crook halted his column at the head of Rosebud Creek for a midmorning rest. Oddly, despite being in hostile Indian country, the general felt no need for extra precautions and failed to post any sentries around his relaxing troopers. Fortunately for the soldiers, Crow and Shoshone scouts attached to Crook's column sensed the enemy's presence nearby and ranged ahead into the pine-covered ridgeline to take a look. At about 8:30 A.M., they sighted a group of Crazy Horse's advance scouts.

A Crow fired the first shot, wounding a Lakota, while several other Crows raced back to warn Crook. Return fire from the Lakotas shot two Crows out of the saddle. A bugle blared and war whoops pierced the warm morning air. The soldiers answered the bugle's call and took up defensive positions. Crazy Horse's Lakotas and Cheyennes galloped through a gap in the surrounding hills and thundered down upon Crook's scrambling troopers. The Crow scouts had warned Crook in time for him to avert disaster but a fierce battle ensued.

The Battle of the Rosebud, fought near the present town of Kirby, Montana, raged all morning and on into the afternoon. Amid chaos and confusion, about 750 Sioux and Cheyenne warriors battled approximately 1,300 soldiers and scouts of Crook's Wyoming column for six hours, with neither side able to gain the advantage. The Cheyenne Wooden Leg later described the battle's ebb and flow:

> Until the sun went toward the west there were charges back and forth. Our Indians fought and ran away, fought and ran away. The soldiers and their Indian scouts did the same. Sometimes we chased them, sometimes they chased us.[74]

The Lakotas and Cheyennes fought with uncustomary coordination and discipline, a tribute to their leader Crazy Horse. At one point in the fighting, Crazy Horse personally rallied his warriors in the face of oncoming bluecoats. Riding among a body of retreating Lakotas, Crazy Horse shouted:

> Death is not the enemy! Do not fear it! If we are to die, let us do so with our faces toward the real enemy! The soldiers are that way![75]

Crazy Horse waved his arm toward the soldiers and charged in their direction. His retreating warriors turned their steeds around and followed him. Their countercharge swept the troopers back down into the little valley. Somehow the soldiers managed to regroup and turn back their Indian attackers yet again.

"We Are Soldiers!"

At another point in the conflict, Captain Guy V. Henry took a bullet in the face. The bullet pierced his left cheek, destroyed the sight in his left eye, and exited

Indian warriors charge U.S. troopers during the fierce Battle of the Rosebud on June 17, 1876.

his right cheek. Blood spurted from his mouth "by the handful" [76] and he toppled from his horse. The Lakotas galloped in to count coup (perform individual acts of valor, such as touching or scalping a victim, while exposing oneself to immediate danger) on the fallen captain. Luckily for Henry, a party of whooping Crow and Shoshone scouts ran them off. Plenty-coups, a Crow chieftain, recalled the rush to rescue Henry:

> Our war whoop, with the Shoshones', waked the Echo-people [Spirits]! We rode *through* them, over the body of one of Three-stars' chiefs who was shot through the face under the eyes, so that the flesh was pushed away

from his broken bones. Our charge saved him from being finished and scalped. [77]

Later, after troopers had borne Henry off to a safe refuge near the crest of a hill, John F. Finerty, a correspondent for the *Chicago Times*, tried to comfort the stricken captain.

The captain simply said, "It is nothing. For this we are soldiers!" [78] Henry then, wrote the mildly amazed reporter, "did me the honor of advising me to join the army." [79] The captain's cool battlefield demeanor at Rosebud was not out of character. Henry had earned the Medal of Honor at Cold Harbor during the Civil War.

The Battle "Where the Girl Saved Her Brother"

In another act of personal heroism, Calf Trail Woman, a warrior, dashed to the aid of Chief Comes in Sight when his horse was shot out from under him. The horseless chief was surrounded by the enemy and had begun his death song (a personal song given to a warrior by a spirit to inspire courage in the warrior and serve as his last words). Suddenly, Calf Trail Woman raced down the ridge, crashed through the enemy line, and reached out a hand to the downed warrior. He grabbed it, leaped aboard, and the pair galloped off to safety.

The Other Cavalry

Few soldiers could surpass the skills of the Plains Indians when it came to fighting from astride a horse. War correspondent Robert E. Strahorn of Denver's Rocky Mountain News *described the other side's cavalry with clear admiration.*

"Some of the most reckless feats of [horseback riding] imaginable were performed by them within range of the broadsides of an entire company. In numerous instances one or two warriors dashed out from behind their cover of rocks, hugged close to the neck of a pony and half bounded, half tumbled down the nearly vertical banks after a bold Crow, Snake [Shoshone] or white skirmisher, delivered a shot or two and like a flash disappeared in spite of volleys sent after them.

Up hill or down, over rocks, through canyons and in every conceivable dangerous condition of affairs their breakneck devil-may-care riding was accomplished. One reckless brave got badly pressed by the cavalry, at a certain point in the field, and jerking out his bowie knife he slashed apart his saddle girt, slipped it with all its trappings from under him while his pony was at full speed, and thus unencumbered made his escape. So closely did the Indians approach our skirmishers at times that they inflicted several wounds from battle-axes, lances and arrows, and in one or two instances they closed in upon a brave soldier and got his scalp before comrades could rush forward to the rescue. They repeatedly courted death by endeavoring to secure the bodies of their own dead."

In her daring rescue of Chief Comes in Sight, Calf Trail Woman—who would later become the only woman to fight against Custer at the Little Bighorn—had saved the life of her brother. Because of her gallantry, the Cheyennes would for all time refer to their clash with Crook at Rosebud Creek as the battle "Where the Girl Saved Her Brother."[80]

Altered History

Both sides took a beating at Rosebud Creek before the Indians broke off the fighting at 2:30 P.M. and turned for home. Because his soldiers had seemingly driven the Indians from the field, Crook reported, "The command finally drove the Indians back in great confusion."[81] But the Indians apparently felt no sense of having been "driven" off the field of battle.

John Stands in Timber, whose grandparents were followers of Sitting Bull, was asked years later why the Indians had withdrawn after appearing to be doing well. He answered with simple eloquence: "They were tired and hungry, so they went home."[82]

Although Crook claimed a great victory, the facts do not support his claim. In dead, the Sioux lost thirteen scalps to their Crow and Shoshone foes and the bluecoats killed seven more. Many more Sioux were wounded. The Cheyennes lost one dead and carried off a number of badly wounded warriors. Crook's Wyoming column lost nine killed and twenty-three wounded. His Crow and Shoshone allies lost one dead and seven wounded.

In terms of numbers alone, it would seem reasonable to say that the Battle of the Rosebud ended in a draw. Beyond question, however, the true victory, both tactical and strategic, belonged to Crazy Horse's warriors. Against a much larger force, they had held their own, mounted charge after charge, and pressured Crook's column into a defensive posture throughout the fighting. They had also inflicted a telling number of casualties on the bluecoats, who came to kill them. Moreover, in successfully protecting their camp and families from destruction at Crook's hands, the Indians emerged from the battle with even more confidence in their ability to defeat the white man's soldiers.

Unknown to the Indians at the time, their repeated attacks and demonstrated ferocity in hand-to-hand encounters so unsettled Three Stars that he would not actively campaign against them again until heavily reinforced. Crook's casualties forced him to limp back to his base camp at Goose Creek to reorganize and resupply his battered column at a most critical time in the campaign. He would not venture forth again for another six weeks. By then, the course of the campaign and history would be everlastingly altered.

Heartbeats

Although present at the Rosebud, Sitting Bull had not taken an active role in the fighting. Fifty half-healed wounds in each arm (from his religious ritual several days earlier) had rendered him incapable of wielding a weapon. Nevertheless, the revered Sioux leader had made his presence felt by continually exposing himself to danger while lending encouragement to his warriors.

A view of Sitting Bull's camp prior to the Battle of the Little Bighorn. The camp quickly swelled to over seven thousand members of the Sioux and Cheyenne nations.

After the battle, Sitting Bull and his followers continued moving westward and set up camp with about 450 lodges along a stream that the Indians called Greasy Grass. The camp doubled in size within a week (to more than seven thousand people, eighteen hundred warriors, in five tribal circles of Sioux and one of Cheyennes), as reservation Indians joined Sitting Bull at the stream known to soldiers as the Little Bighorn.

On June 18, the Indians celebrated their success at the Rosebud and looked forward to "soldiers falling into camp." By then, of course, General Sheridan's three-pronged offensive, so long in the planning, had been reduced to two columns. The time for validating Sitting Bull's vision of a great victory over the soldiers was drawing closer with every Indian heartbeat.

Dust of Uncertain Destiny

Meanwhile, unaware of Crook's retreat, General Terry's column had linked up with Colonel John Gibbon at the mouth of the Rosebud on June 21. Terry gathered

Last Letters

On June 22, 1876, before departing from camp at the junction of the Yellowstone and Rosebud Rivers in Montana Territory, George "Autie" Custer dashed off a hurried letter to his beloved Libbie. He seemed almost boyishly proud of showing off the confidence that General Terry had placed in him. The letter contained nothing of his usual tendency toward affectionate passages. This letter was to be his last.

"My Darling—I have but a few minutes to write as we start at twelve, and I have my hands full of preparations for the scout. Do not be anxious about me. . . .

I send you an extract from Genl. Terry's official order, knowing how [you] keenly appreciate words of commendation and confidence in your dear Bo: 'It is, of course, impossible to give you any definite instructions in regard to this movement, and were it not impossible to do so the Department Commander places too much confidence in your zeal, energy and ability to wish to impose on you precise orders which might hamper your action when nearly in contact with the enemy.'

Your devoted boy Autie."

A day earlier, an anxious Elizabeth Custer had again demonstrated her exceptional prophetic powers in the following letter:

"Ft. Lincoln, June 21st
My Darling Autie,
. . . I cannot but feel the greatest possible apprehension for your safety on this dangerous scout. Oh, Autie, I feel as if it was almost impossible for me to wait your return with patience. I cannot describe my feelings. I have felt so badly for the last few days, I have been practically unendurable to everyone. Most of the time I have spent in my room, feeling myself no addition to any one's society.

. . . Please look after yourself, my darling—not for me alone, but for the country we love and honor.

And now I shall go to bed and dream of my dear Bo. God be with you, my darling. I love you always.

Your devoted Girl,
Libbie"

General Alfred Terry, commander of the spring campaign, devised a plan to trap the Indians in the Little Bighorn Valley.

the officers of both commands, including Lieutenant Colonel Custer, aboard the Yellowstone steamer *Far West* to discuss campaign strategy. Listening to his commander, Custer must have felt a twinge of disappointment, if not bitterness, for General Sheridan had originally intended to place Custer in command of the Dakota column. If Custer felt inclined toward either emotion, he had only himself to blame.

Custer had been called east in March 1876 to testify at congressional hear-ings probing possible misconduct in the scandal-ridden Grant administration. Beyond hearsay about rumored misdeeds by officials on the frontier, Custer had little to contribute to the investigations. But he challenged the wrath of President Grant by implicating the involvement of Grant's brother Orvil in an Indian graft scheme.

A furious President Grant answered Custer's accusations by removing Custer from command of the Dakota column and from participation in General Sheridan's spring campaign. Only after Sheridan again pleaded in Custer's behalf did Grant relent and allow Custer to take part in the outing—but only as a subordinate to General Terry. By then, Custer was delighted to settle for command of his own Seventh Cavalry.

Aboard the *Far West*, Terry explained to his commanders that an earlier scouting party led by Major Marcus A. Reno had tracked an Indian trail forty-five miles up the Rosebud. Then, in anticipation of finding the Indians in the upper valley of the Little Bighorn, Terry outlined a plan to trap the Indians between two columns in a classic pincer movement. He ordered Custer and his Seventh Cavalry to proceed up the Rosebud, cross to the Little Bighorn, and move down the valley from the south. Gibbon and Terry were to complete the movement by marching up the Yellowstone and Bighorn Rivers, effectively blocking the Indians from escaping to the north before closing the pincer on June 26.

On the morning of June 22, with the band playing smartly to the tune of "Garry

Custer leads his column of the Seventh Cavalry south into the Little Bighorn Valley to attack Sitting Bull's camp.

Owen"—Custer's favorite battle song—the Seventh Cavalry, six hundred strong, passed in review for Terry, Gibbon, and Custer. Afterward, Custer, himself a romantic figure in his buckskin jacket and yellow-striped blue trousers, shook hands with his fellow officers and bade them farewell. As Custer galloped off to catch up with his troopers, Terry shouted after him, "Now, Custer, don't be greedy but wait for us."[83]

"No," Custer shouted back, "I will not."[84] The question "Will not what?" has since been asked many times; the answer lies buried beneath the dust of his uncertain destiny.

Another officer recalled, "Little did we think that we had seen him for the last time, or imagine under what circumstances we would next see the command, now mounting the bluffs in the distance with its guidons gayly fluttering in the breeze."[85]

5 First Fight: Reno's Retreat

Custer quickly picked up the Indians' trail and followed it for three days. The trail then turned west and appeared to be much fresher than Custer had expected to find it at that point. A new trail, overridden by reservation Indians, now overlaid the old trail, a clear indication that the Indians were not in the upper valley of the Little Bighorn but much closer at hand.

Terry's Orders to Custer

General Terry had instructed Custer to cross the Little Bighorn Valley in the south to block Indians trying to escape from the upper valley. For well over a century, Terry's orders to Custer have stirred a seemingly endless controversy as to whether Custer followed or disobeyed Terry's instructions. To assure fairness and accuracy, the text of Terry's written order is shown here in its entirety:

> The Brigadier General commanding [Terry] directs that, as soon as your regiment can be made ready for the march, you will proceed up the Rosebud in pursuit of the Indians whose trail was discovered by Major Reno a few days since. It is, of course, impos-

sible to give you any definite instructions in regard to this movement, and were it not impossible to do so the Department Commander [again

Even today, historians argue whether Custer obeyed the orders of his commander during the Battle of the Little Bighorn.

"The Worst That Could Happen"

At twilight on June 22, 1876, the Seventh Cavalry bivouacked twelve miles into the wilderness from the camp at Yellowstone. Custer called his officers together around his campfire, where he informed them of his requirements and expectations for the days ahead.

"We're now starting on a scout we all hope will be successful, and I intend doing everything I can to make it both successful and pleasant for everybody. I'm certain that if any regiment in the service can do what's required of it, we can. I'll be only too glad to listen to suggestions from any officer of this command, if made in the proper manner. But I want it distinctly understood that I'll allow no grumbling, and shall exact the strictest compliance with orders from everybody—not only with mine, but with orders given by any officer to his subordinate. . . .

Only two things will be regulated from my headquarters: when to move out and where to go into camp. All other details on the march will be left to your judgment and discretion. Do what's necessary for your men. This responsibility entails company commanders to keep within supporting distance of each other, not to get ahead of the scouts or very far to the rear of the column.

I want to impress upon you the extent to which I now rely on your judgment, your discretion, your loyalty. Judging from the number of lodges reported by our scouts, we'll meet at least a thousand if not fifteen hundred hostiles. But I feel proudly confident that the 7th Cavalry can whip any number of savages thrown against it. If it can't, no other regiment in the service can. But to win, we need complete harmony in our ranks; and I'm sure we have it. Nothing more, gentlemen, except that marches will be from twenty-five to thirty miles a day. . . . I intend to follow the trail and hunt 'em down even if it takes us into Nebraska. . . . We can't get "Injuns" without hard riding, and plenty of it! That's why I'm depending on you young officers. The worst that could happen is for Sitting Bull to slip away from us just when we've got him roped."

As the ill-fated Indian-fighter was about to learn, Sitting Bull's escape was not "the worst that could happen."

Terry] places too much confidence in your zeal, energy and ability to wish to impose on you precise orders which might hamper your action when nearly in contact with the enemy. He will, however, indicate to you his own views of what your action should be, and he desires that you should conform to them *unless you shall see sufficient reasons for departing from them* [emphasis added]. He thinks that you should proceed up the Rosebud until you ascertain definitely the direction in which the trail above spoken of leads. Should it be found (as it appears almost certain it will be found) to turn toward the Little [Big] Horn, he thinks that you should still proceed southward, perhaps as far as the headwaters of the Tongue, and then turn toward the Little [Big] Horn, feeling constantly, however, for your left, so as to preclude the possibility of the escape of the Indians to the south or southeast by passing your left flank. The column of Colonel Gibbon is now in motion for the mouth of the Big Horn. As soon as it reaches that point it will cross the Yellowstone and move up at least as far as the forks of the Big and Little Horns. Of course, its future movements must be controlled by circumstances as they arise, but it is hoped that the Indians, if upon the Little [Big] Horn, may be so nearly enclosed by the two columns that their escape will be impossible.

The Department Commander desires that on your way up the Rosebud you should thoroughly examine the upper part of Tullock's Creek, and that you should endeavor to send a scout through to Colonel Gibbon's column, with information of the results of your examination. The lower part of this creek will be examined by a detachment from Colonel Gibbon's command. The supply steamer will be pushed up the Bighorn as far as the forks of the river if found to be navigable for that distance, and the Department Commander, who will accompany the column of Colonel Gibbon, desires you to report to him there not later than the expiration of the time for which your troops are rationed, unless in the meantime you receive further orders.[86]

Now certain that the Indians could not be that far away, Custer elected to depart from Terry's plan. On the evening of June 24, he decided to pause for a day, scout the area, locate the Indian camp, then attack on June 26. By then, he figured, Terry and Gibbon would be in position to the north.

Did Custer Disobey Orders?

Custer buffs and historians still argue whether Custer disobeyed orders in departing from Terry's plan. Supporters of the long-haired Indian fighter point to the passage in Terry's Letter of Instructions[87] (as his orders became known) that stated: "the Department Commander places too much confidence in your zeal, energy and ability to wish to impose on you precise orders which might hamper your action when nearly in contact with the enemy."

Custer's detractors refute the foregoing passage. They instead call attention to the passage that starts with: "He will, however, indicate his own views of what your action should be, and he desires that you should conform to them." Custer's critics maintain that in military phrasing a commander's wish or "desire" constitutes a direct order. This is generally true and thus gives rise to the controversy.

Perhaps the eminent Custer historian John S. Gray best resolved the argument when he wrote:

> Terry's instructions contain one tiny word, usually ignored, that made it impossible for Custer's actions to have constituted a violation. This key word is italicized in the following passage: "you should conform to them unless *you* shall see sufficient reason[s] for departing from them." Terry thus explicitly authorized *Custer* to act as the sole judge—not Terry nor any other officer, not some barracks lawyer nor a court-martial, not even history. Only Custer. Period. One may quarrel with Custer's judgement, but not his authority to judge. Custer's obedience is therefore neither debatable, nor relevant.[88]

The logic and lucidity of Gray's declaration would seem more than sufficient to affirm that Custer acted within proper authority.

Custer's Decision

Shortly after daybreak on June 25, Custer's scouts reported sightings of a large herd of Indian ponies and several smoke trails rising out of the Little Bighorn Valley. When several troopers later spotted hostile Indians watching them from the high ground overlooking their column, Custer realized that he had lost the all-important element of surprise. Moreover, with ongoing scouting reports, he grew convinced that the Indian force was much larger than he had anticipated initially.

Custer then faced a dilemma: If he withdrew and the Indians escaped, he would reap the blame; if he attacked, he would be risking all in the face of an unknown and probably superior Indian force, a full day before Terry and Gibbon moved into position. During the Sioux campaign of 1876, the army's main difficulties lay not in defeating the Indians but rather in finding them and forcing them to stand and fight. The Indians' elusiveness no doubt strongly influenced Custer's thinking.

Also, a lack of major military intelligence further hampered Custer. The Bureau of Indian Affairs had led him to believe that he would be facing about eight hundred hostile warriors; in truth, he would encounter about three times that number. Unknown to Custer, the Indians possessed Winchester repeating carbines, while his own men were equipped with single-shot Springfields. Nor had he known of the Indians' growing rage and determination to resist the army's new elimination policy toward so-called hostiles.

In sum, Custer had been either misinformed or uninformed about his enemy in three vital areas: strength of numbers, armament, and willingness to fight. Such lapses hardly enhanced Custer's chances for making sound decisions under pres-

Although Custer used scouts (pictured) to help track the Indians during the campaign, he was unable to determine their exact manpower or position.

sure. In a vale of clouded circumstances, Custer decided to *attack.*

Custer's Orders to Benteen

Given what he knew at the time, Custer's decision held more merit than at first it might seem. Traditionally, cavalry units with superior discipline and firepower had often engaged and defeated much larger groups of Indians. In Custer's out-spoken opinion, the Seventh Cavalry could whip any group of Indians that dared to cross its path—anywhere, anytime. He might have proved it at the Little Bighorn had he not separated his command into three groups—each ultimately incapable of supporting the other—in the face of a much larger Indian force.

Custer did not know the exact strength and location of the Indians, or anything about the nature of the terrain on which he would have to fight. These were things that he had meant to explore on June 25 before attacking on June 26. The nearness of his enemy now forced him to seek this vital information at the same time that he was advancing to the attack—in short, a reconnaissance in force. While continuing to push forward, he split his column into three groups that he could use—separately or together, as dictated by the unfolding tactical situation—in reconnaissance, maneuver, or battle.

Custer first sent Captain Frederick W. Benteen with three troops (companies) to the high ground left and south of the main column, where they could scan the valley. That would also enable Benteen's battalion to prevent the Indians from slipping away to the south. After reconnoitering the valley, Benteen, unless engaged by

Immediately before the Battle of Little Bighorn, Custer sent Captain Frederick W. Benteen (pictured) and his battalion on a reconnaissance mission to determine the location of Sitting Bull's camp.

Indians, was to rejoin Custer and report his findings.

Benteen, a loyal and dedicated regular army officer, but one who made no secret of his contempt for Custer, later expressed displeasure with the assignment. Before a board of inquiry, he referred to Custer's orders as "valley hunting *ad infinitum*"[89] (that is, without end). Benteen went on to voice further criticisms:

> From my orders, I might have gone twenty miles without finding a valley. Still, I was to go on to the first valley, and if I didn't find any Indians, I was to go on to the next valley. Those were the exact words of my order—no interpretation at all. . . . We knew there were eight or ten thousand Indians on the trail we were following. . . .

> But through the whole oblique to the left [maneuver], the impression went with me that all of that hard detour was for nought, as the ground was too awfully rugged for sane Indians to choose to go that way to hunt a camp—or, for that matter, to hunt anything else but game.

> I knew that I had to come to some decision speedily, when I had given up the idea of further hunting for a valley being thoroughly impregnated with the belief that the trail Custer was on would yield quite a sufficiency of Indians. . . . My real, Simon-pure, straight orders were to *hunt that valley;* but I didn't know where the valley was, and thought that perhaps an opportunity might happen later to search for it. . . . So, shouldering the responsibility of not having found the valley, I pitched off with the battalion at a right oblique

to reach the trail Custer's column had followed.[90]

Meanwhile, while Benteen's battalion was coursing over about eight to ten miles of rugged terrain, Custer proceeded northward with his weakened column in the general direction of the Indian camp.

Custer's Orders to Reno

At about 2:30 P.M., Custer and the remainder of his regiment reached a stream—later named Reno Creek—and followed it for about ten miles. Suddenly, about forty warriors galloped off ahead of the column and headed for the Little Bighorn Valley. To the right of the fleeing Indians, an enormous cloud of dust arose from behind a distant ridgeline.

Custer then ordered Major Marcus A. Reno—with three more troops (112 men)—to pursue the Indians across the Little Bighorn River and attack the Indian camp from the south (but north of Benteen). Custer instructed Reno to "move forward at as rapid a gait as you think prudent, charge the village, *and we will support you.*" Reno understood Custer to mean that he (Reno) would "be supported by the whole outfit [the remainder of Custer's Seventh Cavalry]."[91] In the meantime, Custer elected to proceed along a high ridge with the main column—five troops and 210 men—to circle the camp and attack it from the north.

Reno gave chase and made first contact with the Indians at 3:00 P.M. In full view of the Indians, Reno's troops rode into the valley and straight at the village of teepees.

Surprises

Reno's troopers surprised the Indians momentarily. Trooper William Slaper later described his first experience under the gun:

> Soon commenced the rattle of rifle fire, and bullets began to whistle about us. I remember that I ducked my head and tried to dodge bullets which I could hear whizzing through the air. This was my first experience under fire. I know that for a time I was frightened, and far more so when I got my first glimpse of the Indians riding about in all directions, firing at us and yelling and whooping like incarnate fiends [that is, fiends of human form and nature], all seemingly naked as the day they were born.[92]

Low Dog, an Oglala chief, later recounted his sense of disbelief at the moment the soldiers attacked:

> I was asleep in my lodge at the time. The sun was about noon (pointing with his finger). I heard the alarm, but I did not believe it. I thought it was a false alarm. I did not think it possible that any white men would attack us, so strong as we were. We had in camp the Cheyennes, Arapahoes, and seven tribes of the Teton Sioux [Lakotas]—a countless number. Although I did not believe it was a true alarm, I lost no time getting ready. When I got my gun and came out of my lodge the attack had begun at the end of the camp where Sitting Bull and the Uncpapas [Hunkpapas] were. The Indians held their ground to give the women and children time to get out of the way.[93]

The Indians recovered quickly and started fighting back. It then became the Indians' turn to surprise, as they started banging away at the troopers with Winchester repeating rifles.

Some experts believe that the Winchester was superior to the Springfield single-shot rifles used by the soldiers; other experts disagree. Historian Earl A. Brininstool characterized the Springfield as "antiquated . . . with a shell extractor which was not reliable at all."[94] In a more recent evaluation of the rifles, Brian C. Pohanka, a noted Custer authority, contended: "As long as tactical cohesion was retained, the Springfield was superior in both range and stopping power to the lever-action Henry and Winchester rifles."[95] In any case, the Indians surprised the troopers with their rapid-fire capability and fine marksmanship.

River of Blood

Irrespective of the comparative merits of arms, Reno soon realized that his troops would not survive where they were and ordered them to pull back across the river to the high ground to the east. A decade later, with ordered structure and concise descriptions, Reno recorded his remembrances of their withdrawal:

Major Marcus A. Reno and his troops stormed Sitting Bull's camp from the south of the Little Bighorn Valley, taking the Indians by surprise. The Indians' speedy retaliation forced Reno and his men to retreat to higher ground.

A Precarious Situation

Vastly outnumbered and under heavy fire south of Sitting Bull's camp, Major Marcus A. Reno ordered his troopers to remount from their line of skirmishers and withdraw to higher ground. Trooper William C. Slaper, of Troop M, Seventh Cavalry, later recounted his experiences during Reno's retreat across the Little Bighorn on June 25, 1876.

"I cannot say that the retreat from the river bottom—and further on—had a very military appearance, but I can say that I saw nothing disorderly about it, although so many had gone on ahead of me and were so far in advance that what they did, or in what order they retreated, I cannot say with positive certainty. I did not strike the river at the regular ford, so was compelled to jump my horse into the stream at a point where the bank was about six to eight feet high. My animal nearly lost his footing when he struck the water. . . .

As I urged my horse through the water I could see Indians in swarms about the ford above me, and many lashing their ponies to reach that spot, paying no attention to me. One reason for this was that I was alone, and they were doubtless looking for bigger game. Bullets were cutting the air all about me, however, as there were Indians on both banks, as well as in the water, fighting hand-to-hand with the troopers. Death seemed to ride on every hand [everywhere], and yet a kind Providence must have been watching over me, for I crossed the stream unscathed. It was at the ford crossing where many of the men met their death, but in the retreat to the river and the climb up the steep bluffs on the opposite side, some twenty-nine troopers were killed.

I believe one reason why so many of the men escaped was because of the intense dust which was raised by the horses and ponies of the combatants. It hung in dense clouds, and it was almost impossible to see fifty feet ahead in any direction. With fully twenty-five hundred or three thousand Indians racing their ponies about through the dust-laden plain, one can better understand the explanation of the situation. . . .

I arrived at the crest of the hill without even a scratch. . . . I was, however, considerably worried about the rest of the command, and where Custer was and why he had failed to support us as he had promised to do."

I mounted my command and charged through the reds [Indians] in a solid body. As we cut our way through them, the fighting was hand to hand and it was instant death to him who fell from his saddle, or was wounded. As we dashed through them, my men were so close to the Indians that they could discharge their pistols right into the breasts of the savages, then throw them away and seize their carbines, not having time to replace their revolvers in their holsters. . . . Our horses were on the dead run with, in many instances, two and three men on one animal. We plunged into the Little Big Horn and began the climb of the opposite bluffs. This incline was the steepest that I have ever seen horse or mule ascend. . . . In this narrow place (the ford) there were necessarily much crowding and confusion and many men were compelled to cling to the horses' necks and tails for support, to prevent their being trampled to death or falling back into the river. Into the mass of men and horses, the Indians poured a continuous fire and the [L]ittle Big Horn was transferred into a seeming river of human blood.[96]

After the battle, Reno fell heir to much criticism, even charges of cowardice, for his failure to storm the Indian village and for what many felt was his premature withdrawal. Yet, had he continued into the village, it now seems clear that he and his command would have suffered the same fate as did Custer and his battalion later that afternoon. Many of those who survived the fighting at the Little Bighorn owed their lives to Major Reno.

Chapter

6 Custer's Last Battle: A Sad and Terrible Blunder

Custer left Reno and turned right with his remaining five troops—C, E, F, I, and L—and ascended a long gentle slope for about a mile and a half northward, toward the huge cloud of dust rising in the distance. Many historians believe that Custer had intended to move downstream under cover of the bluffs before launching an attack in support of Reno as promised. Custer asked his Crow scout White Man Runs Him what the dust cloud meant. "The Sioux must be running away,"[97] the Crow replied.

Custer and Mitch Boyer, his half-breed Sioux-French scout, along with four Crow scouts, proceeded to a higher vantage point for a better look. Stretched out below them for several miles lay Sitting Bull's sprawling village of nearly a thousand lodges, harboring perhaps two thousand warriors. And rather than running away, the warriors were thundering southward en masse to engage Reno's comparatively meager force. Custer could see Reno's troops dismounting and forming a line of skirmishers in self-defense.

Custer Calls for Help

Custer returned to his column and summoned his bugler John Martin (Giovanni Martini) and blurted out hurried instructions to the Italian trooper. "Orderly, I want you to take a message to Captain Benteen," Custer snapped. "Ride as fast as you can, and tell him to hurry. Tell him it's a big village, and I want him to be quick, and to bring the ammunition packs."[98] Martin saluted. *"Yessir!"*[99] he said and reined away, only to be halted by Custer's adjutant, William W. Cooke.

"Wait, orderly!" commanded Cooke, a big Canadian with a clipped accent and long sideburns. "I'll give you a message."[100] Realizing that Martin spoke only broken English, and wanting to ensure that Benteen got the right message, Cooke scribbled the following note:

BENTEEN:

COME ON. BIG VILLAGE. BE QUICK. BRING PACKS.

W. W. COOKE.

PS BRING PACS [sic].[101]

In his haste to send Martin on his way, Cooke omitted a crucial word from his message, which undoubtedly should have read, "Bring *ammunition* packs." Trooper Martin departed immediately to deliver the urgent message. He therefore survived the impending battle to become

The note Lieutenant William W. Cooke hurriedly scribbled, paraphrasing Custer's plea for help from Captain Benteen.

the last man to see George Armstrong Custer alive.

To ensure prompt delivery of the vital ammunition, Captain Tom Custer, commanding C Company, sent Sergeant Daniel A. Kanipe on the back trail with orders for Captain Thomas M. McDougall to rush forward with the pack train. Both men managed to get through to their destination but to no subsequent avail.

Where Is Benteen?

Custer now found himself in unfamiliar territory, with his regiment split into four parts: the five companies under his direct command; Reno's battalion, already fully engaged and withdrawing to the south; Benteen patrolling to the southwest; and McDougall's pack train with spare ammu-

nition and escort troop farther yet to the south. All four parts now stood exposed and in peril of separate defeats before Custer could reunite them. What happened to Custer and his immediate command from this point forward will doubtless always remain uncertain and the subject of continuing speculation and analyses.

Custer probably intended to find a break in the bluffs along the river that would enable him to cross the Little Bighorn and attack the village from the north. With Reno attacking from the south, and reinforced by Benteen's three companies, Custer could then close the claws of a classic pincer movement. He apparently deployed his immediate forces with this in mind.

By then, Custer had reached a ravine later named Medicine Tail Coulee. Three miles to his west, Medicine Tail Coulee joined with Deep Coulee, another ravine that sliced in from the north and ran into the Little Bighorn at a wide, easy crossing. The major action took place in these two ravines and on the ridges and hills that separated them.

Custer first sent Captain George W. Yates's two-company battalion (E and F Companies) down Medicine Tail to the river. Then, with Captain Myles W. Keogh's three-company battalion (C, I, and L Companies) Custer dismounted his troops and formed a line of skirmishers on the north slope of Medicine Tail. Custer probably intended, with Keogh, to defend Benteen's approach route, while Yates held the river crossing. When Benteen arrived, Custer would then be positioned to thrust into the village. It now became a question of "where is Benteen?"

No More Luck

Because not one soldier with Custer survived the ensuing battle, the details of his infamous last stand must necessarily derive from the scattered recollections of Indians, from hearsay and conjecture, and from more than a century of intensive study and analysis. The sheer enormity of scholarly endeavor directed upon the subject has served only to refine documented suppositions as to what actually happened that hot summer afternoon in the Montana Territory. Owing to the immensity of work available on the battle, only selected glimpses from both sides will be used to reconstruct what is known of Custer's end.

Although Indian eyewitness accounts of the battle have endured by word of mouth, such accounts were not documented until years after the event. Also, Indian participants in the battle tended to focus on individual struggles and failed to illuminate the larger strategic and tactical aspects of the confrontation. Such limitations should not be overlooked when evaluating the reliability and scope of Indian reportage. On the other hand, the

The circumstances surrounding Custer's death and the Seventh Cavalry's last stand are shrouded in mystery. Since all of Custer's soldiers were killed during the battle, little evidence remains to describe their actions on that fateful day.

remembrances of Indian combatants and eyewitnesses have provided valuable insight into Custer's last battle.

The Battle of the Little Bighorn began when Sioux warriors led by a Hunkpapa chief named Gall swarmed across the Little Bighorn River to the attack at approximately 3:45 P.M. While Gall pressed in on Custer from the south, the Oglala chief Crazy Horse descended on the hapless troopers from the north. Low Dog, another Oglala chief, recalled how the fighting started:

Hunkpapa chief Gall gallantly led his Sioux warriors against Custer during the opening salvos of the Battle of the Little Bighorn.

I called to my men, "This is a good day to die: follow me." We massed our men, and that no man should fall back, every man whipped another man's horse and we rushed right upon them. As we rushed upon them, the white warriors dismounted to fire, but they did very poor shooting. They held their horses' reins on one arm while they were shooting, but their horses were so frightened that they pulled the men all around, and a great many of their shots went up in the air and did no harm. The white warriors stood their ground bravely, and none of them made any attempt to get away.[102]

Custer's five companies soon gravitated (or were driven) toward three hills that later became known as Custer Ridge, Battle Ridge, and Calhoun Hill (named for Custer's brother-in-law and commander of L Company, First Lieutenant James Calhoun). Gall's attack forced Yates's battalion back onto Battle Ridge. Calhoun and his men died defending the hill named for him. Crazy Horse then struck at Battle Ridge and the adjacent ravines.

In the end, the remnants of Custer's troops clustered together on Custer Ridge, completely surrounded by Crazy Horse's rolling attack. The troopers shot their horses to form a rough, circular barricade and fought to the last man. Two Moons, a Northern Cheyenne chief, continued the Indian narrative:

Then the Sioux rode up the ridge on all sides, riding very fast. The Cheyennes went up the left way. Then the shooting was quick, quick. Pop-pop-pop very fast. Some of the soldiers went down on their knees, some stand-

A painting from 1882 captures Custer and his men in their frenzied last battle.

ing. Officers all in front. The smoke was like a great cloud, and everywhere the Sioux went the dust rose like smoke. We circled all around them— swirling like water around a stone. We shoot, we ride fast, we shoot again. Soldiers drop, and horses fall on them. Soldiers in line drop, but one man rides up and down the line—all the time shouting. He rode a sorrel horse, with white legs and white forelegs. I don't know who he was. He was a brave man.

Indians keep swirling round and round, and the soldiers killed only a few. Many soldiers fell. At last all horses, but five were killed. Once in a while some man would break out and run toward the river, but he would fall. At last about a hundred men and five horsemen stood on the hill all hunched together. All along the bugler kept blowing his commands. . . . And the five horsemen and the bunch of men started toward the river. Then man on sorrel horse led them, shouting all the time. He wore a buckskin shirt and had long black hair and a moustache. . . . One man all alone ran down toward the river, then round up over the hill. I thought he was going to escape, but a Sioux fired and hit him in the head. He was the last man. He wore braid on his arms.[103]

A member of the Seventh Cavalry scrambles to free himself after his horse is killed while another, barricaded behind his fallen horse, fires on the Indians.

In less than an hour, Custer and all of his men lay dead under a blistering afternoon sun. Custer's luck had finally run out.

One Great Victory

Meanwhile, Benteen had received Custer's message. But instead of rushing to Custer's aid, Benteen elected instead to join forces with Reno's column as it withdrew from the Little Bighorn Valley. Even though they plainly heard the sound of firing, indicating that Custer was engaged, neither Reno nor Benteen offered to join the fighting. But Captain Thomas B. Weir, commander of D Company, rode off in the direction of the firing at about 4:55 P.M. Weir's entire company followed after him without orders.

Shocked or shamed into decisive action by Weir's act, Benteen, probably also without orders, followed on the trail of D Company with H, K, and M Companies at about 5:10 P.M. Between 5:30 and 5:40, Weir and Benteen occupied a high hill now named Weir Point. From there, through clouds of smoke and dust, their troopers caught glimpses of Custer's last moments. First Lieutenant Edward S. Godfrey, commander of K Company, reported that "the firing had ceased except for an occasional shot." Second Lieutenant Winfield S. Edgerly, of D Company, said that he "saw many Indians riding around firing at objects on the ground."[104]

Finally, at approximately 5:45 P.M., Reno arrived with the rest of his troops. Almost at once, a large force of Indians returning from the Custer battlefield attacked Reno's entire force again, forcing Reno into another fighting withdrawal to the bluff now known as Reno Hill.

The combined forces of Reno and Benteen then dug in on the southern bluffs and fought off the Indians for the rest of the day. Nightfall brought only temporary relief to the surrounded troopers. At first light, the Indians attacked again and the siege continued until late in the afternoon of June 26.

Benteen, to his credit, personally led a counterattack and threw back the Indians on the south perimeter. Benteen also inspired Reno to mount a similar counter-charge on the opposite side. As the forces of Terry and Gibbon arrived from the north, the Indians finally struck their teepees and withdrew to the south. But not before the Indians had won their one great victory over the U.S. Cavalry. They would not win another.

Benteen's Story

Casualty figures resulting from Custer's "last stand" vary from source to source. For sure, however, Custer lost all of his five companies. The Indians left Custer's body and those of all his soldiers stripped of their clothes and (except for Custer's) scalped, mutilated, and riddled with arrows. Reno and Benteen together lost fifty-three killed and sixty wounded.

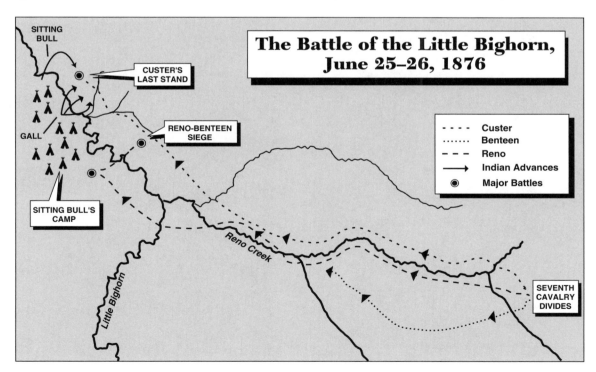

The Battle of the Little Bighorn, June 25–26, 1876

SITTING BULL
CUSTER'S LAST STAND
GALL
RENO-BENTEEN SIEGE
SITTING BULL'S CAMP

- - - - Custer
.... Benteen
– – – Reno
——→ Indian Advances
◉ Major Battles

Reno Creek

Little Bighorn

SEVENTH CAVALRY DIVIDES

Estimates of Indian dead range from thirty to three hundred.

After General Terry arrived, Captain Benteen asked and was granted permission to visit the Custer battleground. Benteen later described his findings:

> I went over the battlefield carefully, with a view to determine how the battle was fought. I arrived at the conclusion I have right now—*that it was a rout, a panic, till the last man was killed; that there was no line formed.*
>
> There was no line on the battlefield. You can take a handful of corn and scatter it over a floor, and make just such lines. There were none. The only approach to a line was where five or six horses were found at equal distances, like skirmishers. Ahead of them were five or six men at about the same distances, showing that the horses were killed, and the riders jumped off, and were heading to get where Custer was. *That was the only approach to a line on the field.* There were more than twenty killed there to the right; there were four or five at one place, all within a space of twenty to thirty yards. *That was the condition all over the field.*

In the aftermath of the Battle of the Little Bighorn, an Indian warrior triumphantly holds the scalp of a dead soldier. In addition to scalping, the victors also stripped the dead soldiers of their clothing and mutilated their bodies.

After the battle, one of the Indian survivors produced this sketch of the Little Bighorn battlefield. Naked soldiers litter the ridge, many of them headless and disfigured.

Only where General Custer was found was there any evidence of a stand. The five or six men I spoke of were where Capt. Calhoun's body was; they were of his company. There were twenty-two bodies found in a ravine, fifty to seventy-five yards from the river. They had, I think, been killed with stones and clubs. They were unarmed; I think they were wounded men who had gone into the ravine to hide. There was a trail leading to a crossing about a hundred yards above the ravine.

I counted seventy dead horses and two Indian ponies. I think, in all probability, that the men turned their horses loose without any orders to do so. Many orders might have been given, but few obeyed. *I think that they were panic-stricken; it was a rout, as I said before.*[105]

A Prayerful Petition

A petition circulated and signed by nearly all of the surviving members of the Seventh Cavalry provides additional evidence that Major Marcus A. Reno conducted himself properly at the Little Bighorn.

"We, the enlisted men, the survivors of the battle on the heights of the Little Big Horn, on the 25th and 26th of June, 1876, of the Seventh Regiment of Cavalry, who subscribe our names to this petition, most earnestly solicit the President and Representatives of our country, that the vacancies among the commissioned officers of our Regiment, made by the slaughter of our brave, heroic, now lamented, Lieut.-Col. George A. Custer, and the other noble dead commissioned officers of our Regiment . . . be filled by the officers of the Regiment only. That Major M. A. Reno be our lieutenant-colonel, vice [in place of] Custer killed; Capt. F. W. Benteen be our major, vice Reno promoted. . . . Your petitioners know that this is contrary to the established rule of promotion, but prayerfully solicit a deviation from the usual rule in this case, as it will be conferring a bravely-fought-for and a justly-merited promotion on officers who, by their bravery, coolness and decision on the 25th and 26th of June, 1876, saved the lives of every man now living of the Seventh Cavalry who participated in the battle, one of the most bloody on record, and one that would have ended with the loss of every officer and enlisted man on the field, only for the position taken by Major Reno, which we held with bitter tenacity against fearful odds, to the last.

To support this assertion—had our position been taken one hundred yards back from the brink of the heights overlooking the river, we would have been entirely cut off from water; and from beyond those heights, the Indian demons would have swarmed in hundreds, picking off our men by detail, and before mid-day, June 26th, not an officer or enlisted man of our Regiment would have been left to tell of our dreadful fate, as we would have been completely surrounded."

When considering Benteen's story, it should be remembered that it was he who stood over Custer's corpse and said to Reno:

> There he is, God dam him! He'll never fight anymore. You know enough of me to know I'd have gone through to him if it was possible to do so. But anyhow, I'm only too proud to say I hated him.[106]

Some students of the Little Bighorn clash think that had Benteen hurried he might have made it through to Custer's be-

In 1879 a military board of inquiry vindicated Major Reno for his actions during the Battle of the Little Bighorn.

sieged forces and saved the doomed soldiers. Other scholars believe that had Benteen made it through his troops would have met death along with Custer's. The debate will ever remain unwinnable.

Field of Glory

Benteen's assessment of Custer's final battle as "*a rout, a panic, till the last man was killed*" did not go unchallenged. A military board of inquiry was held in Chicago in 1879 to investigate charges brought against Major Reno for failing to go to Custer's aid. In summarizing the prosecution's case, court recorder Lieutenant Jesse M. Lee wrote in part:

> The well-known capacity, tenacity and bravery of Gen. Custer and the officers and men who died with him forbid the supposition of a panic and a rout. There was a desperate and sanguinary [bloodthirsty] struggle in which the Indians must have suffered heavily. From the evidence that has been spread before this court it is manifest that Gen. Custer and his comrades died a death so heroic that it has but few parallels in history. Fighting to the last and against overwhelming odds, they fell on the field of glory. Let no stigma of rout or panic tarnish their blood-bought fame. Their deeds of heroism will ever live in the hearts of the American people, and the painter and the poet will vie with each other in commemorating the world-wide fame of Custer and his men.[107]

The board upheld Major Reno's actions and conduct at the Little Bighorn and absolved him of charges. Lieutenant Lee's summation remains in the record.

Precious Cargo

On June 30, 1876, fifty-two wounded survivors of the Reno-Benteen siege were either marched or carried to the *Far West*, then located fifty-three miles from the mouth of the Little Bighorn, and loaded safely aboard the steamer. General Terry conferred with Grant Marsh, the *Far West*'s captain, and was reported to have said:

Captain, you are about to start on a trip with fifty-two wounded men on your boat. This is a bad river to navigate and accidents are liable to happen. I wish to ask of you that you use all the skill you possess, all the caution you can command, to make the journey safely. Captain, you have on board the most precious cargo a boat ever carried. Every soldier here who is suffering with wounds is the victim of a terrible blunder; a sad and terrible blunder.[108]

Remembrances

Of the innumerable controversies spawned at the Little Bighorn, perhaps none was debated more hotly than the actions of Major Reno and Captain Benteen. Perhaps both officers deserve remembrance and deliverance in a manner implied by the esteemed Custer historian William A. Graham, when he wrote:

> The charges against Reno and Benteen [of disloyalty, disobedience of orders, and failure to go to Custer's relief] took added strength from the known enmity of both men toward Custer; but it is as unthinkable as it is untrue that these officers deliberately sacrificed more than two hundred comrades, members of their own regiment, because of their unfriendly feeling toward their commander: for that, in plain terms, was the charge against them in the final analysis. There is nothing in the history of the fight on the Little Big Horn which justifies such a charge; it ought never to have been made, much less believed. On the contrary, while Reno did not show himself to be a great commander who could rise above the demands of trying and desperate conditions, it was due to his withdrawal from the valley, by whatever cause inspired, and to Benteen's heroic leadership, that any of the Seventh Cavalry survived. The [Reno] court of inquiry found nothing that required animadversion [adverse criticism], and such was its unanimous report to the President.[109]

As for the central figure in one of history's dominant controversies, Brevet Major General George Armstrong Custer, perhaps no words serve his memory better than those of Lieutenant James H. Bradley of the Seventh Infantry. After viewing the general's body on Custer Hill, surrounded by his comrades-in-arms, Bradley wrote:

> Probably never did a hero who had fallen upon the field of battle appear so much to have died a natural death. His expression was rather that of a man who had fallen asleep and enjoyed peaceful dreams than of one who had met his death amid such fearful scenes as that field had witnessed, the features being wholly without ghastliness or any impress of fear, horror or despair. He had died as he lived, a hero.[110]

The Hows and Whys

The hows and whys of that classic encounter at the Little Bighorn will doubtlessly long continue to fire the imaginations of historians and military buffs. For thoughtfulness coupled with simplicity, few summaries of that event can compare with that offered by the preeminent Custer scholar John S. Gray.

"The 7th Cavalry had clearly suffered a disastrous defeat. As to how it happened there is no mystery whatever. The regiment of 31 officers and 566 men tackled two thousand warriors resolved to defend their women and children and their tribal existence. Man for man, the brave was a more skillful fighter than the soldier. [About 40 percent of the soldiers were little more than raw recruits.] The regiment was divided into four columns, only two of which attempted attacks, and then at separate times and places, each, therefore, against crushing odds. It was a classic defeat in detail.

But why had Custer attempted so much with so little? The ultimate reason was simply inadequate enemy intelligence. Custer, like Terry and Gibbon, underestimated both the strength and temper of the Indians. Up to the very last minute, the evidence Custer was so [busily] gathering seemed to conceal the true strength of the hostiles, and to indicate that they were in flight. Yet, Custer was keener on intelligence than his fellow-officers. . . .

But why did Custer not keep his regiment together? He tried to, but could not afford the delay necessary to achieve it. He detailed more men than he could spare [more than eighty] to hurry the pack train along, but it was an amateur outfit. It was Benteen's dawdling, contrary to orders and common sense, that held his battalion out of action. And Custer attacked separately from Reno because he thought the village was in flight, and then terrain features delayed and displaced his attack. What the outcome might have been, if the regiment had been together, no one can say. . . .

Custer's decisions, judged in the light of what he knew at the time, instead of by our hindsight, were neither disobedient, rash, nor stupid. Granted his premises, all the rest follows rationally."

The Seventh Cavalry's valiant last stand continues to be one of history's most intriguing battles.

Many questions about the battle remain unanswered today and likely will never have irrefutable answers. But as long as soldiers heed the bugle's call, one unassailable fact about the clash will endure: Out of defeat and death, Custer reserved for himself and the Seventh Cavalry a permanent place of honor in the history and folklore of two great cultures.

Warriors of the Lakotas claimed that "only the rocks and mountains last forever; men must die."[111] While it is true that all men must die, the deeds of some men transcend their mortality. Such were the deeds of Custer and the Seventh Cavalry. Their legend will last as long as a single storyteller remains to repeat it—perhaps even as long as the rocks and mountains.

Notes

Introduction: The Last Great Indian Victory

1. Edward S. Godfrey, *Custer's Last Battle*, in Paul Andrew Hutton, ed., *The Custer Reader*. Lincoln: University of Nebraska Press, 1992, pp. 310–11.

Chapter 1: Washita: Son of the Morning Star

2. Quoted in Alan Axelrod, *Chronicle of the Indian Wars: From Colonial Times to Wounded Knee*. New York: Prentice Hall, 1993, p. 205.

3. Quoted in Robert M. Utley and Wilcomb E. Washburn, *The American Heritage History of the Indian Wars*. New York: Barnes & Noble, 1977, p. 244.

4. Quoted in Axelrod, *Chronicle of the Indian Wars*, p. 205.

5. Quoted in Axelrod, *Chronicle of the Indian Wars*, p. 206.

6. Quoted in Axelrod, *Chronicle of the Indian Wars*, p. 206.

7. Quoted in Axelrod, *Chronicle of the Indian Wars*, p. 207.

8. Utley and Washburn, *The American Heritage History of the Indian Wars*, p. 244.

9. Quoted in D. A. Kinsley, *Custer, Favor the Bold: A Soldier's Story*. New York: Promontory Press, 1992, p. 387.

10. Quoted in Kinsley, *Custer, Favor the Bold*, p. 388.

11. Quoted in Kinsley, *Custer, Favor the Bold*, p. 388.

12. Quoted in Kinsley, *Custer, Favor the Bold*, p. 388.

13. Quoted in Kinsley, *Custer, Favor the Bold*, p. 388.

14. General George Armstrong Custer, *My Life on the Plains*. New York: Carol Publishing Group, 1993, p. 216.

15. Quoted in Maguerite Merington, ed., *The Custer Story: The Life and Letters of General George A. Custer and His Wife Elizabeth*. New York: Barnes & Noble, 1994, p. 217.

16. Quoted in E. Lisle Reedstrom, *Custer's 7th Cavalry: From Fort Riley to the Little Big Horn*. New York: Sterling, 1992, p. 50.

17. Quoted in Jeffry D. Wert, *Custer: The Controversial Life of George Armstrong Custer*. New York: Simon and Schuster, 1996, pp. 271–72.

18. Quoted in Wert, *Custer*, p. 270.

19. Quoted in Kinsley, *Custer, Favor the Bold*, p. 390.

20. Quoted in Kinsley, *Custer, Favor the Bold*, p. 390.

21. Quoted in Kinsley, *Custer, Favor the Bold*, p. 390.

22. Quoted in Kinsley, *Custer, Favor the Bold*, p. 390.

23. Quoted in Merington, *The Custer Story*, p. 217.

24. Custer, *My Life on the Plains*, p. 283.

25. Custer, *My Life on the Plains*, p. 319.

26. Custer, *My Life on the Plains*, p. 319.

27. Quoted in Kinsley, *Custer, Favor the Bold*, p. 393.

28. Custer, *My Life on the Plains*, pp. 321–22.

29. Custer, *My Life on the Plains*, p. 322.

30. Quoted in Kinsley, *Custer, Favor the Bold*, p. 395.

31. Custer, *My Life on the Plains*, p. 331.

32. Evan S. Connell, *Son of Morning Star.* New York: Promontory Press, 1984, p. 184.

33. Quoted in Utley and Washburn, *The American Heritage History of the Indian Wars*, p. 256.

34. Quoted in Connell, *Son of Morning Star*, p. 184.

35. Quoted in Connell, *Son of Morning Star*, p. 185.

36. Quoted in Reedstrom, *Custer's 7th Cavalry*, p. 56.

37. Custer, *My Life on the Plains*, p. 356.

38. Quoted in Custer, *My Life on the Plains*, p. 389.

Chapter 2: Custer: From Bull Run to the Black Hills

39. Quoted in Merington, *The Custer Story*, p. 12.

40. Quoted in Merington, *The Custer Story*, p. 13.

41. Quoted in Kinsley, *Custer, Favor the Bold*, p. 71.

42. Quoted in Merington, *The Custer Story*, p. 56.

43. Quoted in Merington, *The Custer Story*, p. 55.

44. Quoted in Kinsley, *Custer, Favor the Bold*, p. 134.

45. Quoted in Kinsley, *Custer, Favor the Bold*, p. 134.

46. Quoted in Gregory J. W. Urwin, *Custer: The Civil War Years*, in Hutton, *The Custer Reader*, pp. 15–16.

47. Quoted in Urwin, *Custer*, p. 16.

48. Quoted in Urwin, *Custer*, p. 17.

49. Quoted in Urwin, *Custer*, p. 17.

50. Quoted in Wert, *Custer*, p. 192.

51. Quoted in Urwin, *Custer*, p. 17.

52. Quoted in Urwin, *Custer*, pp. 18–19.

53. Quoted in Merington, *The Custer Story*, p. 101.

54. Quoted in Urwin, *Custer*, p. 21.

55. Quoted in Urwin, *Custer*, p. 23.

56. Quoted in Merington, *The Custer Story*, p. 159.

57. Quoted in Kinsley, *Custer, Favor the Bold*, p. 335.

58. Quoted in Brian W. Dippie, *Custer: The Indian Fighter*, in Hutton, *The Custer Reader*, p. 108.

59. Quoted in Kinsley, *Custer, Favor the Bold*, p. 443.

60. Quoted in Reedstrom, *Custer's 7th Cavalry*, p. 97.

61. Quoted in Reedstrom, *Custer's 7th Cavalry*, p. 98.

Chapter 3: Sitting Bull: Soldiers Falling into Camp

62. Quoted in Utley and Washburn, *The American Heritage History of the Indian Wars*, p. 266.

63. Quoted in Kinsley, *Custer, Favor the Bold*, p. 468.

64. Quoted in Kinsley, *Custer, Favor the Bold*, p. 468.

65. Quoted in John S. Gray, *Centennial Campaign: The Sioux War of 1876*. Norman: University of Oklahoma Press, 1988, p. 29.

66. Quoted in Gray, *Centennial Campaign*, p. 31.

67. Quoted in Axelrod, *Chronicle of the Indian Wars*, p. 222.

68. Quoted in Gray, *Centennial Campaign*, p. 94.

69. Quoted in Gray, *Centennial Campaign*, pp. 94–95.

70. Quoted in Robert M. Utley, *The Lance and the Shield: The Life and Times of Sitting Bull.* New York: Henry Holt, 1993, pp. 133–34.

71. Quoted in James Welch with Paul Stekler, *Killing Custer: The Battle of the Little Bighorn and the Fate of the Plains Indians.* New York: W. W. Norton, 1994, p. 51.

Chapter 4: Last Farewell: On to the Little Bighorn

72. Quoted in Robert Kammen, Joe Marshall, and Frederick Lefthand, *Soldiers Falling into Camp: The Battles at the Rosebud and the Little Big Horn.* Encampment, WY: Affiliated Writers of America, 1992, p. 3.

73. Quoted in Kammen, *Soldiers Falling into Camp,* p. 3.

74. Quoted in Utley, *The Lance and the Shield,* p. 141.

75. Quoted in Kammen, *Soldiers Falling into Camp,* p. 9.

76. Quoted in Wayne Michael Sarf, *The Little Bighorn Campaign: March–September 1876.* Conshohocken, PA: Combined Books, 1993, p. 110.

77. Quoted in Sarf, *The Little Bighorn Campaign,* p. 110.

78. Quoted in Connell, *Son of Morning Star,* p. 90.

79. Quoted in Sarf, *The Little Bighorn Campaign,* p. 111.

80. Quoted in Welch, *Killing Custer,* p. 121.

81. Quoted in Gray, *Centennial Campaign,* p. 123.

82. Quoted in Sarf, *The Little Bighorn Campaign,* p. 113.

83. Quoted in Wert, *Custer,* p. 336.

84. Quoted in Wert, *Custer,* p. 336.

85. Quoted in Edgar I. Stewart, *Custer's Luck.* Norman: University of Oklahoma Press, 1955, p. 253.

Chapter 5: First Fight: Reno's Retreat

86. Quoted in Gray, *Centennial Campaign,* pp. 147–48.

87. Charles Kuhlman, *Legend into History* and *Did Custer Disobey Orders at the Battle of the Little Big Horn?* Mechanicsburg, PA: Stackpole Books, 1994, p. 22.

88. Gray, *Centennial Campaign,* p. 148.

89. Quoted in Bruce A. Rosenberg, *Custer and the Epic of Defeat.* University Park: Pennsylvania State University Press, 1974, p. 30.

90. Quoted in Rosenberg, *Custer and the Epic of Defeat,* pp. 30, 32.

91. Quoted in E. A. Brininstool, *Troopers with Custer: Historic Incidents of the Battle of the Little Big Horn.* Mechanicsburg, PA: Stackpole Books, 1994, pp. 16, 167.

92. Quoted in Rosenberg, *Custer and the Epic of Defeat,* p. 33.

93. Quoted in Rosenberg, *Custer and the Epic of Defeat,* p. 33.

94. Brininstool, *Troopers with Custer,* p. 29.

95. Brian C. Pohanka, Preface to Brininstool, *Troopers with Custer,* p. xx.

96. Quoted in Rosenberg, *Custer and the Epic of Defeat,* p. 37.

Chapter 6: Custer's Last Battle: A Sad and Terrible Blunder

97. Quoted in Gray, *Centennial Campaign,* p. 174.

98. Quoted in Brininstool, *Troopers with Custer,* p. 189.

99. Quoted in Kinsley, *Custer, Favor the Bold,* p. 529.

100. Quoted in Brininstool, *Troopers with Custer,* p. 189.

101. Quoted in Sarf, *The Little Bighorn Campaign,* p. 213.

102. Quoted in Utley and Washburn, *The American Heritage History of the Indian Wars*, p. 273.

103. Quoted in Rosenberg, *Custer and the Epic of Defeat*, pp. 40–41.

104. Quoted in Gray, *Centennial Campaign*, p. 180.

105. Quoted in Brininstool, *Troopers with Custer*, pp. 84–85.

106. Quoted in Kinsley, *Custer, Favor the Bold*, p. 537.

107. Quoted in Rosenberg, *Custer and the Epic of Defeat*, p. 55.

108. Quoted in Stewart, *Custer's Luck*, p. 481.

Epilogue: Remembrances

109. W. A. Graham, *The Story of the Little Big Horn: Custer's Last Fight*. Mechanicsburg, PA: Stackpole Books, 1994, pp. 103–104.

110. Quoted in Graham, *The Story of the Little Big Horn*, p. 109.

111. Quoted in Richard Erdoes and Alfonso Ortiz, eds., *American Indian Myths and Legends*. New York: Pantheon Books, 1984, p. 467.

Glossary

Appomattox: Appomattox Courthouse; a little town in Virginia where Generals Grant and Lee signed an agreement to end the Civil War.

Arapaho: Plains tribe of the Algonquian peoples living in eastern Colorado and southeastern Wyoming.

battalion: A body of troops made up of headquarters and two or more companies or batteries.

bayonet: A steel blade attached to the muzzle of a rifle for use in hand-to-hand fighting; first used in Bayonne, France, in the seventeenth century.

Blackfoot: A northern plains tribe of northwestern Montana.

breechloader: A firearm loaded from its breech.

brevet: A rank higher than that for which a military officer receives pay; similar to an acting (temporary) appointment in present-day services.

Brulé: A division of the Lakota.

Cheyenne: A nomadic, buffalo-hunting tribe of the Algonquian peoples of the northern and central plains.

Colt .44: A revolving six-shooter invented by Samuel Colt; it became the West's most popular pistol.

Comanche: A Shoshonean tribe of Indians inhabiting the central and southern Great Plains.

company: A military unit consisting usually of a headquarters and two or more platoons.

count coup: Indian phrase meaning to perform individual acts of valor, such as touching or scalping a victim, while exposing oneself to immediate danger.

Dakota: The Eastern Sioux, living primarily east of the Missouri River.

demerit: A mark signifying a lack of merit, usually entailing a loss of privilege to an offender.

division: A tactical combat unit or formation larger than a regiment or brigade but smaller than a corps.

Dog Soldier: The Hotamitanio; a member of an elite warrior clique among the Cheyenne and various other tribes of the western plains; principal duties consisted of policing tribal activities, such as ceremonies, hunts, and raiding parties.

forage: Food for animals, especially when taken by grazing.

garrison: A permanent military installation.

Greasy Grass: Indian name for the Little Bighorn River.

hostiles: The government's term for Indians who refused the Indian Office ultimatum to come into the reservation by January 31, 1876.

Hunkpapa: A division of the Lakota.

Kiowa: A Uto-Aztecan tribe of Indians living primarily in the southern plains.

Lakota: The Western Sioux, living primarily west of the Missouri River; also known as the Teton Sioux (*see also* Teton Sioux).

Manifest Destiny: A concept shared by many Americans during the nineteenth century that the United States was destined by divine right to expand its national boundaries to accommodate an ever-increasing population.

Miniconjou: A division of the Lakota.

muzzle loader: A firearm loaded from its discharging end.

nontreaties: The government's term for Indians who opted to live independently off the reservation.

Oglala: A division of the Lakota or Western Sioux.

regiment: A military unit larger than a battalion and smaller than a division.

Sans Arc: A division of the Lakota.

scalp: The custom of cutting off part or all of the scalp of an enemy as a token of victory.

Sioux: The Indians who call themselves Dakota.

skirmish line: A line of soldiers in advance of a battle line.

Spencer carbine: A .52- or .56-caliber, lever-action, repeating rifle invented by C. M. Spencer; popular in the West during the post–Civil War period.

Springfield rifle: A .45-caliber, side-hammer, single-shot rifle called the "Trap Door"; adopted for army use in 1873.

strategy: The planning and directing of the entire operation of a war or campaign.

tactics: The art of placing or maneuvering forces skillfully in a battle.

Teton Sioux: The largest and most powerful branch of the Dakota Indians (*see also* Lakota).

treaties: The government's term for Indians who consented to living on the reservation.

troop: A cavalry unit corresponding to an infantry company; the terms *troop* and *company* are often used synonymously.

Wakantanka: Lakota term for Great Medicine or Mystery; a supreme entity or power.

Winchester carbine: A .44-caliber, centerfire, fifteen-shot rifle; it became known as "the rifle that won the West."

wiwanyag wachipi: Lakota religious ceremony; literally, dance looking at the sun (now called the Sun Dance).

For Further Reading

Michael Antonucci, "Island of Death," *Command Magazine,* January/February 1994. A brief, interesting account of the Battle of Beecher's Island in 1868, where some seven hundred Indian warriors held fifty-one army scouts under siege for eight days at the Arikara Fork of the Republican River in Colorado.

John M. Carroll, ed., *They Rode with Custer: A Biographical Directory of the Men That Rode with General George A. Custer.* Mattituck, NY: J. M. Carroll, 1993. Short biographies of the men of Seventh U.S. Cavalry, described by the book's editor as "the clothes and buttons of the men who rode with Custer."

R. Ernest Dupuy and Trevor N. Dupuy, *The Encyclopedia of Military History.* New York: Harper & Row, 1977. A monumental work on warfare by two noted military historians; includes a brief outline of events occurring before, during, and immediately after the Battle of the Little Bighorn.

Richard Allen Fox Jr., *Archaeology, History, and Custer's Last Battle: The Little Bighorn Reexamined.* Norman: University of Oklahoma Press, 1993. The author uses innovative and standard archaeological techniques, combined with Indian eyewitness accounts and historical documents, to vividly replay Custer's last battle in astonishing detail.

Paul Andrew Hutton, ed., *Soldiers West: Biographies from the Military Frontier.* Lincoln: University of Nebraska Press, 1987. A collection of fourteen short biographies emphasizing "the wide diversity of style, temperament, activity, and occupation that marked the careers of frontier soldiers"; includes informative pieces on Philip H. Sheridan, George Crook, Nelson A. Miles, and George A. Custer.

David Humphreys Miller, *Custer's Fall: The Native American Side of the Story.* New York: Penguin Books, 1992. The story of the worst defeat ever inflicted by Native Americans on the U.S. Cavalry; written from a Native American viewpoint and based on the author's twenty-two years of research and on the oral testimony of seventy-two Native American eyewitnesses.

Clyde A. Milner II, Carol A. O'Connor, and Martha A. Sandweiss, eds., *The Oxford History of the American West.* New York: Oxford University Press, 1994. A panoramic view and masterful retelling of America's move west.

Craig Philip, *Last Stands: Famous Battles Against the Odds.* Greenwich, CT: Dorset Press, 1994. A compelling volume that spans the centuries to re-create famous battles as varied as Thermopylae, Vicksburg, and Dien

Bien Phu; includes an excellent chapter on "the sharp little action that took place around the Little Bighorn River on 25 June 1876."

Mari Sandoz, *Crazy Horse: The Strange Man of the Oglalas.* Lincoln: University of Nebraska Press, 1992. A sensitive biography of the great Oglala chief, "whose personal power and social nonconformity set him off as 'strange'"; and who led the Sioux in many battles, including the clash at the Little Bighorn.

Works Consulted

Alan Axelrod, *Chronicle of the Indian Wars: From Colonial Times to Wounded Knee.* New York: Prentice Hall, 1993. A sweeping narrative of the Indian Wars from the time the Europeans first landed in America until their final confrontation with the Indians at Wounded Knee.

Winfred Blevins, *Dictionary of the American West.* New York: Facts On File, 1993. This remarkable dictionary lists "5,000 Terms and Expressions, from 'a-going and a-coming' to Zuni"; recaptures the unique language of the American West and provides enjoyable, informative reading from cover to cover.

Cyrus Townshend Brady, *The Sioux Indian Wars: From the Powder River to the Little Big Horn.* New York: Barnes & Noble, 1992. An exhaustive history of the clash between the two very different cultures of red man and white; contains many true stories that, in Brady's words, "speak for themselves . . . and ring like a trumpet call."

E. A. Brininstool, *Troopers with Custer: Historic Incidents of the Battle of the Little Big Horn.* Mechanicsburg, PA: Stackpole Books, 1994. Although all those under Custer's immediate command at the Little Bighorn perished, other participants (under Reno and Benteen) in the battle survived; author Brininstool investigates and reports their stories, often in their own words.

Evan S. Connell, *Son of Morning Star.* New York: Promontory Press, 1984. Author Connell "explores deeply the personalities of Custer and the other federal and Indian leaders," while re-creating "an era from our past that haunts us still."

Elizabeth B. Custer, *Boots and Saddles or: Life in Dakota with General Custer.* 1885. Reprint, Williamstown, MA: Corner House Publishers, 1977. Mrs. Custer's own fascinating account of life on remote frontier outposts with her famous soldier-husband.

General George Armstrong Custer, *My Life on the Plains.* New York: Carol Publishing Group, 1993. The personal narrative of the most famous cavalry leader in American history, covering the major part of his life; originally published two years before the general's death at the Little Bighorn.

Richard Erdoes and Alfonso Ortiz, eds., *American Indian Myths and Legends.* New York: Pantheon Books, 1984. One hundred and sixty-six legends drawn from the heart and soul of the native people of North America, tales some of which have been told for thousands of years, while others have been reshaped and refitted to meet their listeners' changing needs.

W. A. Graham, *The Story of the Little Big Horn: Custer's Last Fight.* Mechanicsburg, PA: Stackpole Books, 1994. The first book-length history of the Battle of the Little Bighorn, published fifty years after the event; an authoritative sourcebook that gave root to many newer works chronicling this ever-popular subject.

John S. Gray, *Centennial Campaign: The Sioux War of 1876.* Norman: University of Oklahoma Press, 1988. A soundly documented and engrossing book that presents a total view of the U.S. Army campaign against the Sioux in 1876; written by a retired medical doctor and professor of physiology who is also the author of some forty articles and three other books on western history.

——, *Custer's Last Campaign: Mitch Boyer and the Little Bighorn Reconstructed.* Lincoln: University of Nebraska Press, 1991. The author uses all known primary accounts of the Little Bighorn battle and employs topographic research in conjunction with time-motion analysis to piece together a clear picture of heretofore clouded events; arguably the finest single volume available on Custer's famous stand at the Little Bighorn.

Paul Andrew Hutton, ed., *The Custer Reader.* Lincoln: University of Nebraska Press, 1992. A compilation of articles depicting George Armstrong Custer as seen by himself, his peers, and leading scholars. These pieces offer a rounded insight into the many sides of the man who became the subject of enormous admiration, controversy, and myth.

Robert Kammen, Joe Marshall, and Frederick Lefthand, *Soldiers Falling into Camp: The Battles at the Rosebud and the Little Big Horn.* Encampment, WY: Affiliated Writers of America, 1992. A look at the crucial battles at the Rosebud and Little Bighorn as told from a Native American point of view; blends oral accounts handed down by Sioux and Crow participants with U.S. Army records of the battles.

D. A. Kinsley, *Custer, Favor the Bold: A Soldier's Story.* New York: Promontory Press, 1992. Author Kinsley "sympathetically captures the whole of Custer's personality: his tempestuous and brilliant military career, his tender love for his wife Libbie, his explosive temperament, and his awful self-indulgence in gaming with his Fate."

Charles Kuhlman, *Legend into History* and *Did Custer Disobey Orders at the Battle of the Little Big Horn?* Mechanicsburg, PA: Stackpole Books, 1994. Kuhlman concentrates on the intriguing unknowns of Custer's last battle—the how and why rather than the what and when; the volume includes the author's sixty-four-page defense of Custer's actions.

Howard R. Lamar, ed., *The Reader's Encyclopedia of the American West.* New York: Harper & Row, 1977. A broad but detailed view of western history; contains more than twenty-four hundred entries examining "the people, places, institutions, and ideas that collectively define the American frontier experience." This volume belongs on the bookshelf of anyone truly interested in learning more about the American West.

Maguerite Merington, ed., *The Custer Story: The Life and Letters of General George A. Custer and His Wife Elizabeth.* New York: Barnes & Noble, 1994. The story of Custer's deeply personal and devoted relationship with his beloved wife Elizabeth; history charmingly portrayed through the letters of two people very much in love with each other.

Clyde A. Milner II, Carol A. O'Connor, and Martha A. Sandweiss, eds., *The Oxford History of the American West.* New York: Oxford University Press, 1994. A comprehensive compendium that combines the work of twenty-eight historians to render full treatment to the rich complexities of this vast region.

E. Lisle Reedstrom, *Custer's 7th Cavalry: From Fort Riley to the Little Big Horn.* New York: Sterling, 1992. An authentic account of George Armstrong Custer's Seventh Cavalry—its post–Civil War uniforms, weapons, equipment, and much more—prepared by a respected historian and western illustrator.

Bruce A. Rosenberg, *Custer and the Epic of Defeat.* University Park: Pennsylvania State University Press, 1974. An English professor at Pennsylvania State University explores the making of a legend and compares the actual events surrounding Custer's stand at the Little Bighorn with the myths about it that have since been developed in American folklore.

Wayne Michael Sarf, *The Little Bighorn Campaign: March–September 1876.* Conshohocken, PA: Combined Books, 1993. The author describes the personalities and events that preceded the Custer disaster at the Little Bighorn and examines the nature of Indian fighting on the Great Plains; the weapons used, the forces involved, and the strategies and tactics employed by army troopers and Indian warriors.

Edgar I. Stewart, *Custer's Luck.* Norman: University of Oklahoma Press, 1955. A remarkable book that presents graphically and on a broad canvas the great and not-so-great events that led to, and culminated at, that memorable clash at the Little Bighorn.

Robert M. Utley, *The Lance and the Shield: The Life and Times of Sitting Bull.* New York: Henry Holt, 1993. A vivid historical biography that corrects many misconceptions about Sitting Bull—one of the nation's greatest Native Americans; written by a former chief historian of the National Park Service and author of many distinguished works of history and biography.

Robert M. Utley and Wilcomb E. Washburn, *The American Heritage History of the Indian Wars.* New York: Barnes & Noble, 1977. An impressive volume that covers four hundred years of bloody conflict between the Indians and their white conquerors; written by two noted authorities on Indian culture and affairs.

Peter Watts, *A Dictionary of the Old West 1850–1900.* New York: Wings Books, 1977. This singularly American dictionary "explains and preserves all the colorful, distinctive words and phrases used by cattle ranchers, miners, cowpunchers, scouts, trappers, gamblers, and other Westerners in the heyday of the Old West"; a totally enjoyable reference source of the colorful western idiom.

James Welch with Paul Stekler, *Killing Custer: The Battle of the Little Bighorn and the Fate of the Plains Indians.* New York: W. W. Norton, 1994. The first nonfiction work of James Welch, the acclaimed Native American novelist; written in collaboration with documentary filmmaker Paul Stekler, it is "a poignant and highly personal resurrection of the Indian side of the story from beneath a mountain of myth and misinterpretation."

Jeffry D. Wert, *Custer: The Controversial Life of George Armstrong Custer.* New York: Simon and Schuster, 1996. The author reexamines the events of the Seventh Cavalry's defeat at the Little Bighorn, "drawing on recent archaeological findings and the latest scholarship," to put the performances of Custer and his subordinates in proper perspective.

Index

Apache Indians, 13, 27
Arapaho Indians, 13, 17, 27
Ayers, Lorenzo, 51

Bacon, Elizabeth. *See* Custer, Elizabeth Bacon
Barnitz, Albert, 23, 25–26
Battle of the Little Bighorn, 67–88
Custer and
orders of, 71–73
sends for help, 77–78
Benteen joins Reno instead, 82–83
Terry's orders to, 67–69
disobeyed, 69–71
map, 83
military board of inquiry about, 87–89
Reno's surprise attack, then retreat, 73–76
slaughter at, 79–82
strategy meeting on the *Far West*, 62–65
wounded transported on the *Far West*, 88
Battle of the Rosebud, 55–62
Battle of the Washita, 16–17, 22–30
attack, slaughter, retreat, 23, 25–30
Custer and
account of, 27

honored and condemned for, 41
map, 25
plan of attack, 22–23
Beauregard, Pierre G. T., 33
Belknap, William W., 48
Bell, James M., 26–27
Benteen, Frederick W.
at Battle of the Little Bighorn, 72–90
blamed for loss, 90
Custer and
orders to, 71–73
sends for help to, 77–78
joined Reno, not Custer, 82–83
views on, 83–85
at Washita, 25–27
Bingham, John A., 31, 33–34
Black Hills Expedition, map of, 44
Black Kettle (Cheyenne chief), 16
at Battle of the Washita 26–27, 41
Black Moon (cousin of Sitting Bull), 53
Boyer, Mitch, 77
Boy General with the Golden Locks (Custer), 36
Bozeman Trail, 12, 14
War for, 13
Bradley, James H., 89

Brady, Mathew, 34
brevet rank, 19, 36
Bridger, Jim, 20
Brininstool, Earl A., 74
Bull Bear (Dog Soldier chief), 16

Calf Trail Woman (Cheyenne), 60–61
Calhoun, James, 80, 85
California Joe, 23
Chandler, Zachariah, 48
Chapman (Union general), 37
Cheyenne Indians, 13–15, 27
attacks on white settlements, 12, 17
see also named battles
Cheyenne-Arapaho War, 16
Chicago Times, 59
Chief Comes in Sight (Cheyenne), 60
children, Indian in battle, 26, 27
Civil War
Custer's experience in, 33–39
Commanches, 13–14
at Washita, 27
Cooke, William W., 77–78
count coup, 59
Crawford, Samuel J., 19
Crazy Horse (Lakota chief), 52

at Battle of the Rosebud, 55–62
Crittenden, John J., 32
Crook, George, 49–51
    at Battle of the Rosebud, 55–62
Crow Indians, 48, 55, 58, 60–61
Custer, Elizabeth Bacon, 19, 35
    correspondence with Custer, 20, 36, 63
    marriage of, 36
Custer, George Armstrong
    as author
        correspondence with wife, 20, 36, 63
        letter of appreciation to troops, 40
        magazine articles for *Galaxy*, 40–41
        My Life on the Plains, 24, 42
        on Battle of the Washita, 27
        on destruction of Indian ponies, 27–28
        on Indian scouts, 24
    as Boy General with the Golden Locks, 36
    Civil War experience, 33–39
        appointed as youngest general, 36
        commendation and promotion by Sheridan, 39
        "Custer's Luck," 38
    early life
        at West Point, 31–32
        birth, 31
        education, 31–32
        political stance, 38
    post–Civil War activities, 15–22, 39–44
        as Son of the Morning Star, 23
        court-martial and suspension of, 18, 41
        reinstatement of, 18–19, 41
        early forays against Indians, 12
        map of expeditions, 44
        testimony against Grant's brother, 64–65
        winter campaign of, 15–22
        Yellowstone and other expeditions, 42–44
        map of, 44
    see also Battle of the Little Bighorn; Battle of the Washita
Custer, Thomas Ward, 26, 78

Dakota Territory, 42–44
    gold rush in, 44–45
Denver Rocky Mountain News, 49, 60
Dog Soldiers (Hotamitanio), 14–15
    described, 16

Early, Jubal A., 39
Edgerly, Winfield S., 82
Elliott, Joel H., 21–22, 26, 29–30
Emancipation Proclamation, 38

Far West (steamboat), 88

prebattle strategy meeting on, 64–65
Finerty, John F., 59
Forsyth, George A., 15
Fought, Joseph, 33

Galaxy magazine, 40–41
Gall (Hunkpapa chief), 80
"Garry Owen" (marching song), 25, 30, 65–66
Gibbon, John, 50–51, 62, 66, 69
"Girl I Left Behind Me, The" (marching song), 21
Godfrey, Edward S., 11, 82
gold rush, in Dakota, 44–45
Graham, William A., 89
Grant, Orvil, 64
Grant, Ulysses S., 39
    approved plan to destroy Indians, 18, 46–48
Gray, John S., 70, 90
Great Sioux Reservation, 46–47
    established, 13–14
    map of, 14

Hale, Owen, 26
Hamilton, Alexander, 25
Hamilton, Louis, 23, 25
Hancock, Winfield Scott, 12, 41
    Hancock's Campaign, 13
Hard Rope (Indian tracker), 22
Hayfield Fight, 12
He Dog (Oglala chief), 50, 55
Henry, Guy V., 58–59

Hooker, Joseph, 35
Hotamitanio. *See* Dog
 Soldiers
Howard, Jacob M., 38
Hunkpapa Indians. *See*
 Sioux Indians

Indians. *See individual tribes*
Indian Territory, 13

John Stands in Timber
 (Cheyenne), 57, 61
Johnston, Joseph E., 34

Kanipe, Daniel A., 78
Keogh, Myles W., 78
Kiowa Indians, 13–14, 27

Lakota Indians. *See* Sioux
 Indians
Laramie Treaty of 1868,
 13–14
 map, 14
Lee, Jesse M., 87–88
Lee, Robert E., 36–37, 39
LeForge, Tom, 16
Lincoln, Abraham, 35
 Emancipation Proclama-
 tion and, 38
Little Beaver (Indian
 tracker), 22
Little Bighorn. *See* Battle
 of the Little Bighorn
Low Dog (Oglala chief),
 73, 80

Manifest Destiny, 47
maps
 Battle of the Little
 Bighorn, 83
 Battle of the Washita, 25
 Custer's expeditions of
 1873–74, 44

Laramie Treaty of
 1868, 14
Sheridan's spring cam-
 paign, 52
Marsh, Grant, 88
Martin, John (Giovanni
 Martini), 77
McClellan, George B.,
 34–35
McDougall, Thomas M., 78
McLean, Wilmer, 39
Medicine Lodge Treaty of
 1867, 13, 17
Merritt, Wesley, 37
My Life on the Plains
 (Custer), 24, 42

New York Herald, 36
New York Times, 29
Northern Pacific Railroad,
 42

Old Bear (Cheyenne
 chief), 50, 55
Osage Indians, 23

Pawnee Indians, 16
Pleasonton, Alfred, 35–36
Plenty-coups (Crow chief),
 59
Pohanka, Brian C., 74
Powder River
 U.S. defeat at, 50–51

Reno, Marcus A., 65
 at Battle of the Little
 Bighorn, 73–89
 blamed for loss of, 89
 Custer's orders to, 73
 surprise attack, then
 retreat by, 73–76
 troops' petition for, 86
Reynolds, Joseph J., 50–51

rifles. *See under* weapons
Rosebud, Battle of, 55–59

Schofield, John M., 17–18
scouts
 Indian, 58, 77
 described, 24
 white, 23
Sheridan, Philip Henry,
 14–15
 commendation of
 Custer, 39
 disastrous winter
 campaign of, 14–30,
 48–51
 on Custer's success at
 Washita, 30
 on a fair, square fight, 37
 on a good Indian is a
 dead Indian, 18
 Powder River defeat
 of, 50–51
 spring campaign of,
 51–52
 map, 52
 see also Battle of the
 Rosebud
Sherman, William
 Tecumseh, 14
 on Indians' violation of
 treaties, 17–18
 planned destruction of
 Indians, 18
Shoshone Indians, 55, 58,
 60–61
Sioux Indians, 15, 45
 Custer's forays against,
 12
 see also named battles
Sitting Bull (Hunkpapa
 chief), 45
 did not fight at Rose-
 bud, 61

felt called to be holy
man, 53
vision of soldiers falling
into camp, 51–54
see also Battle of the
Little Bighorn
Slaper, William, 73, 75
Smith, Edward P., 48
Son of the Morning Star
(Custer), 23
Star of Washita, 23
St. Louis Democrat, 29
Strahorn, Robert E., 49, 60
Stuart, J. E. B., 35–37
Sully, Alfred, 18–20
Sun Dance ritual, 53–54

Tall Bull (Dog Soldier), 16
Terry, Alfred H., 50–52,
62–66, 84, 88

orders to Custer, 67–69
Custer's response,
69–71
Thieves' Trail, 43
Two Moons (Cheyenne
chief), 80–81

Wade, Ben, 38
Wagon Box Fight, 12
War for the Bozeman
Trail, 13
Watkins, Erwin C., 48
weapons
breech-loaded rifles, 13
Colt .44 revolver, 22
muzzle-loading rifles,
13
Spencer carbine, 22
Springfield single-shot
rifles, 70, 74

Winchester repeating
carbine, 15, 70, 74
Weir, Thomas B., 82
West, Robert M., 23
West Point, Custer at,
31–32
White Horse (Dog
Soldier), 16
White Man Runs Him
(Crow scout), 77
women, Indian, 26, 27
Wooden Leg (Cheyenne),
52, 54, 58

Yates, George W., 78,
80
Yellowstone Expedition,
42–44
map, 44
Young, P. B. M., 32

Picture Credits

Cover photo: Peter Newark's Western Americana

Brown Brothers, 87

Corbis-Bettmann, 54

Culver Pictures, Inc., 33

Courtesy Little Bighorn Battlefield National Monument, 31, 42, 43, 64, 72, 74

Library of Congress, 10, 12, 13, 46, 51, 59, 67, 79, 81

National Archives, 15, 18, 34, 80

North Wind Picture Archives, 28, 56, 65, 71, 91

Photo courtesy of South Dakota State Historical Society—State Archives, 55

Stock Montage, Inc., 21, 50

UPI/Corbis-Bettmann, 36

West Point Museum, U.S. Military Academy, Courtesy Little Bighorn Battlefield National Monument, 78

About the Author

Earle Rice Jr. attended San Jose City College and Foothill College on the San Francisco peninsula, after serving nine years with the U.S. Marine Corps.

He has authored thirteen previous books for young adults, including fast-action fiction and adaptations of *Dracula* and *All Quiet on the Western Front*. Mr. Rice has written several books for Lucent, including *The Cuban Revolution*, *The Battle of Midway*, *The Battle of Belleau Wood*, *The Attack on Pearl Harbor*, and *The Tet Offensive*. He has also written articles and short stories and has previously worked for several years as a technical writer.

Mr. Rice is a former senior design engineer in the aerospace industry who is now a full-time writer. He lives in Julian, California, with his wife, daughter, two granddaughters, four cats, and a dog.